D is for DOG

An Easy Guide to Veterinary Care for Dogs

Dr. Terrie Sizemore DVM

This is a work of non-fiction.
Text and Illustrations copyright
by Terrie Sizemore, DVM, RN ©2016

Library of Congress Control Number: 2016901563

All rights reserved. No part of this book may be reproduced, transmitted, or stored in an information retrieval system in any form or by any means,
graphic, electronic, or mechanical without prior written permission from the author.

First Edition 2016

Printed in the United States of America

A 2 Z Press LLC
PO Box 582
Deleon Springs, FL 32130
bestlittleonlinebookstore.com
bestlittleonlinebookstore@gmailcom
386-681-7402

ISBN: 978-1-9469087-99-5

Dedication

This book is dedicated in
loving memory
of my beloved grandfather,
Alexander Balcziunas.

Table of Contents

Preface ix
Introduction x
Chapter 1: Welcome 1
Chapter 2: The First Few Weeks 9
   Supplies 10
   Puppy-proofing the home 12
   Picking a veterinarian 15
Chapter 3: Vaccines 17
   The major preventable diseases 18
   Transmission of germs 19
   The vaccine controversy 22
   Why vaccinate? 24
   Distemper 26
   Hepatitis 30
   Leptospirosis 32
   Kennel cough (parainfluenza) 37
   Parvo 40
   Corona virus 43
   Bordatella 46
   Rabies 48
   Lyme disease 53
   Special needs for puppies 56
   Adverse reactions to vaccines 59
Chapter 4: Tick diseases 61
   Ehrlichiosis (ur-lick-ee-oh-sis) 63
   Anaplasmosis (an-uh-plaz-moh-sis) 64
   Rocky Mountain Spotted Fever (RMSF) 65
   Hepatozoonosis (hep-at-oh-zo-in-oh-sis) 68
   Babesiosis (baa-bee-zee-oh-sis) 69
   Tick paralysis 70
   Tick removal 71
Chapter 5: Spaying and neutering 73
   Reasons to spay 76
   Reasons to neuter 77
   When to spay and neuter 81
   Complications of spaying and neutering 82
   Ways to minimize complications of spaying and neutering 83
Chapter 6: What to expect when your dog is expecting 85

- Getting pregnant 86
- Yes! We're pregnant! 88
- Benefits of x-rays when pregnant 89
- Being prepared 91
- Stage 1 of puppy delivery 92
- Stage 2 of puppy delivery 93
- Stage 3 of puppy delivery 94
- When to worry 96
- What to do 97
- The puppies are here 98
- Calcium caution 99
- Medications safe for use in pregnant dogs 102
- Medications not safe for use in pregnant dogs 103

Chapter 7: Dental Care 107
- Tooth eruption 108
- Stages of tartar buildup 110
- Signs and symptoms pets need dental care 114
- Reasons for dental care 115
- Preventative care for dental needs 116
- Brushing your pet's teeth 117
- Definitions about dental needs of dogs .... **Error! Bookmark not defined.**

Chapter 8: Nutrition 119
- Stages of development 120
- Types of diets 124
- Weight management diets 125
- Goals for weight management 127
- Body conditioning scores (BCS) 130
- Benefits of lower calorie foods 135
- Treats 136
- Healthy snacks 137
- Homemade treats 138

Chapter 9: Arthritis 145
- Types of arthritis 146
- Signs of arthritis 147
- Goals for pet owners 148
- Treatment for arthritis 149

Chapter 10: Poisons 157
- Signs of poisoning 158

Foods to avoid	159
Household items to avoid	161
Plants and shrubs to avoid	163
What to do if a pet is poisoned	165
Chapter 11: Training	**167**
How to socialize your pets	171
Frequently encountered behavioral issues	176
Chapter 12: Diagnostic testing	**179**
Common tests recommended	180
Heartworm disease	181
Signs of heartworm disease	186
Treating heartworm disease	187
Preventing heartworm disease	188
Fecal tests	189
Common intestinal worms in dogs	190
Roundworms	193
Hookworms	194
Whipworms	196
Tapeworms	198
Giardia and coccidia	201
Bloodwork	202
Facts about blood	204
Complete blood counts	204
Chemistry	206
Electrolytes	208
Pancreas tests	209
Thyroid tests	210
Bile acids	213
Cushing's and Addison's testing	214
Blood clotting testing	218
Diabetic testing	222
X-rays	224
Ultrasound	225
Advanced imaging	226
Skin testing	227
Skin disorders	228
Skin scraping	230
Demodex (mange)	231
Sarcoptic mange	232

Fine needle aspiration and biopsy 233
Allergies 235
Allergy testing 236
Immunotherapy 237
Fleas 238
Food allergy 239
Contact allergies 240
Bacterial hypersensitivity 240
Insect bites 241
Inhalant allergies (atopy) 242
Vaccine and medication reactions 245
Cultures 246
Fungal cultures 247
Urine exams 248
Disorders of the urinary system 249
Urine testing 250
Signs of ear disorders 251
Ear exams 252
Ear care 253
Signs of eye disorders 254
Disorders of the eye 255
Eye examination 256
Staining tests for the eye 257
Tear testing for the eye 258

Chapter 13: Miscellaneous **261**
Lost pets 261
Tips for finding lost pets 262
Microchippiing 264
Emergencies 265
What to do in an emergency 266
Checking a pet's temperature, heart rate and breathing rate 267
First aid kits 270
Doing your own pet exam 271
Senior pets 280
Signs of aging 281
Tips for aging pets 282
Dog ages and sizes 283

PREFACE

The author has been a busy veterinarian for many years and has had the unique experience of meeting people from many backgrounds in her varied practice.

She has observed that pet owners would like to learn, know, feel confident and understand more about pet care for the pets they love and engage with everyday.

It is the intent of the author to create a book that simplifies technical medical information so that the reader becomes informed without being overwhelmed. She hopes to eliminate frustration some owners face and encourages readers and owners to continue their quest for knowledge. She is convinced informed owners make better owners and will make better decisions for their pets.

It is this author's hope not only that every reader enjoys the basic and easy-to-understand information in this book, but that after reading it, they can, with confidence, seek great care for their pets.

This book is written to provide owners with basic general information regarding pet needs and care.

This work is not intended to be a substitute for veterinary care. No one can learn the professional discipline of being a veterinarian from a book. You, as the reader, will quickly realize many disorders overlap in signs and symptoms; and there is caution to not overlook serious illness as much as to not mistake simple, uncomplicated disorders for more serious illness.

Please seek veterinary care for your pet as needed. Some situations you may encounter with your beloved pets require immediate attention.

Enjoy this book!

INTRODUCTION

Every day in my chosen professions, I make technical medical information understandable to my clients and patients. Even some of my dog patients seem to look at me as if they are listening intently and understand everything.

Dogs have many roles in the lives of people. Some are close companions, pets, or furry children. They fill lonely hours for many people as well as making childhood the most memorable time.

Other dogs have professions—some are guide dogs for the visually impaired, some are medical alert dogs for conditions such as diabetes and seizures. Some dogs have roles assisting those with psychiatric or emotional needs, or autism, and some dogs even detect peanut allergies. All these dogs share the reward of allowing more independence for the ones they are born to help.

Dogs have been trained for search and rescue of missing persons and cadavers. They have the unique ability to track people in the wilderness, in hazardous weather, under snow, and even under water.

Dogs assist producers by herding cattle, sheep, reindeer, and fowl. Some are sled dogs, show dogs, mascots, guard dogs, bomb and drug detectors, or cart dogs, and some have served in the military. Others have entertained us for years.

We can all agree dogs truly are man's best friend and we love them. Keeping them healthy and in their chosen professions or with families is what I do every day.

"D is For Dog" provides basic knowledge for every dog owner. The subjects range from vaccines for major preventable diseases in dogs to reasons for spaying and neutering, what to expect when our dogs are expecting, tick diseases, arthritis, dental care, emergency care, performing a physical exam, geriatric concerns, nutritional care for dogs emphasizing overweight management, poisonous substances to dogs, and a very brief chapter on training.

Chapter 1

WELCOME

TO THE WONDERFUL WORLD
OF "WOOF" OWNERSHIP

Whether you found your new best friend:

From a local breeder —

— decided on a designer breed —

— rescued a very lucky pup from an animal shelter —

— or perhaps your precious pup came via a neighbor, friend, or family with unexpected blessings —

Just like the rest of the family, our dogs need the proper nutrition, exercise, love, and medical care.

Veterinarians are also committed to the best care for your pet and are certain you want to understand care recommendations so you as pet owners can make great choices for your furred (and sometimes not furred) friends.

Chapter 2

THE FIRST FEW WEEKS

It is exciting to pick out the toys, the bed, the clothes…

SUPPLIES

- food
- treats
- ceramic or stainless steel bowls (NO PLASTIC PLEASE)
- ID tags
- collars and harnesses
- brushes, combs and dog shampoo

Additional items that may come in handy are:

- clean-up supplies
- stain removers
- paper towels
- deodorizing sprays
- and floor dusters

PUPPY-PROOFING THE HOME

Don't forget to puppy-proof the house by remembering to:

1. Cover electrical cords.
2. Store breakable and precious items where pups cannot damage them.
3. Keep all clothing, nylons, and undergarments from pups.
4. Store poisonous cleaning chemicals out of reach—behind doors with latches (child-proof).
5. Store or remove all chemical fertilizers, herbicides, and insecticides out of reach of your pup.
6. Store auto maintenance chemicals—like gasoline, kerosene, oil, and antifreeze out of reach of your pet.
7. Inspect your yard for holes or gaps in your fence so pups cannot escape.
8. Remove poisonous plants from your home and yard—find a list of common poisonous plants/shrubs in chapter 10.
9. Keep children's toys out of reach—small parts may be swallowed by pups.
10. Cover pools.

And always remind children at home and visiting to be kind and gentle with the pets.

Last but not least:

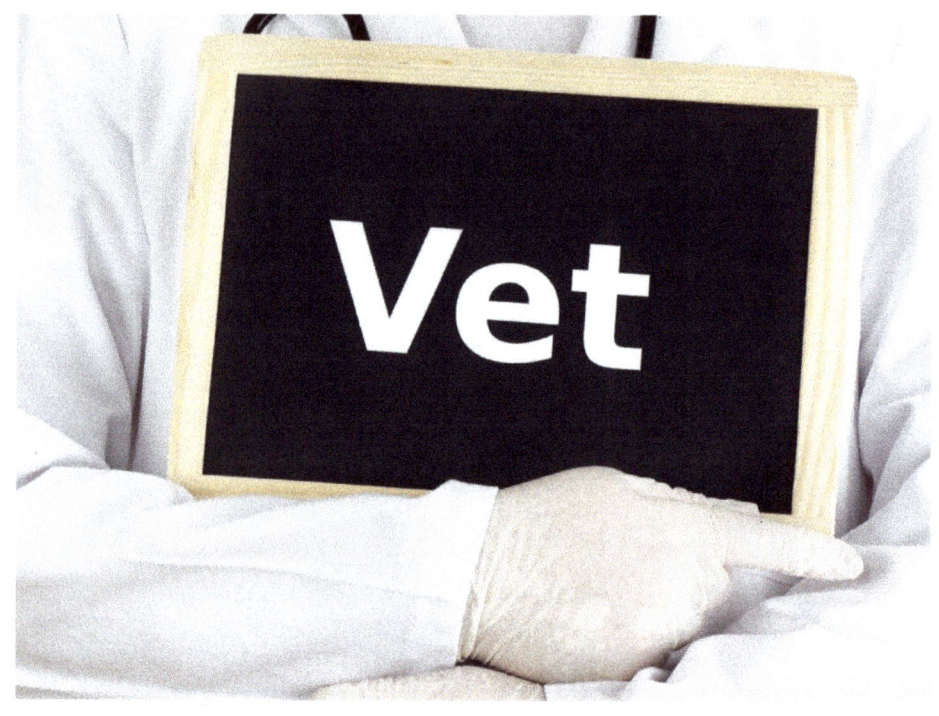

... don't forget to pick a veterinarian!

PICKING A VETERINARIAN

WHAT TO CONSIDER WHEN CHOOSING YOUR PET'S DOCTOR

Some clinics provide
- general service
- some are exclusive or mixed for horses
- some service farm animals
- some are 'cats only'
- some treat birds, fish, reptiles, and exotics

Other clinics have specialists for advanced care for:
- surgical needs
- skin diseases
- bone care
- eye/ear/neuro-logical issues
- and other specialty concerns

NOW THAT WE HAVE WELCOMED OUR PUPS,
SOME BASIC TOPICS OF PET CARE
INCLUDED IN THIS BOOK ARE:

- vaccines
- tick diseases
- spaying and neutering
- what to expect when your dog is expecting
- dental care (teeth)
- nutrition
- pet poisons
- training and behavior
- frequently recommended testing
- heartworms
- pet parasites
- fleas
- and more!

Chapter 3
VACCINES

Many years ago, scientists studied germs and disease. No one believed very small, microscopic 'things'—AKA germs—could enter a person's or pet's body and cause disease.

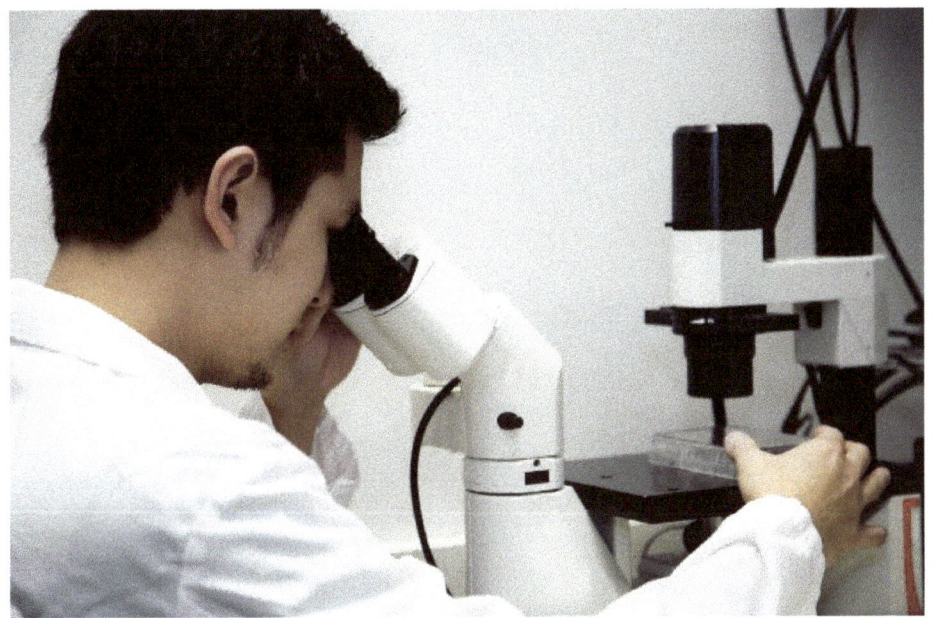

"GERMS" include:
- bacteria
- viruses
- fungi—which includes yeast and molds

THE MAJOR PREVENTABLE DISEASES

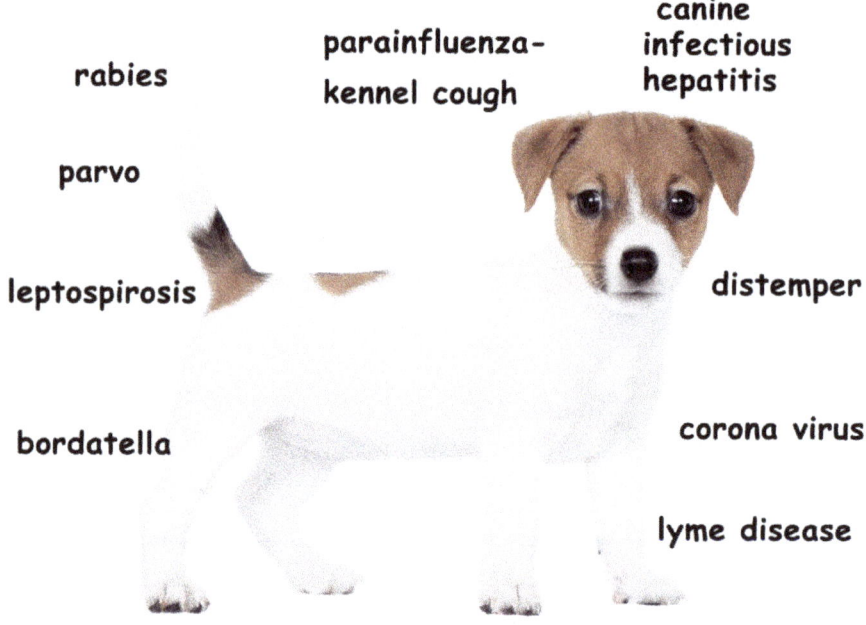

Today more is known about germs and disease. Microscopic organisms do indeed cause diseases that affect our dogs.

TRANSMISSION OF GERMS

Dogs encounter infectious organisms—GERMS—by

- touch—direct contact from dog to dog
- exposure to fecal material, AKA poop
- saliva of infected dogs
- wildlife—such as raccoons, skunks, coyotes and more
- fleas, mosquitoes and ticks
- rodents
- exposure to water—puddles, lakes, and other waterways contaminated with disease-causing germs
- "fomites"—objects that carry germs: like boots, pants legs, backpacks, and other physical objects

Scientists invented vaccines to protect pets from disease.

When well dogs are vaccinated, they make protective proteins called antibodies against the diseases they are vaccinated for. This protection allows them to fight infection if exposed to real germs.

Goals when vaccinating are:
- pets will not become ill,
- or the illness will be mild.

THE VACCINE CONTROVERSY

There has been much controversy over vaccines:

Despite the controversy over vaccinating, and while it is true there are minimal risks to vaccinating dogs,

it is still the number one and best way to minimize or eliminate illness in our dogs.

Vaccinating is not a method of treating illness or a cure for the diseases outlined in the pages to follow, but a means of *preventing* illness.

It has been proven that the risks of disease are far greater than the risks of vaccinating.

WHY vaccinate?

When a dog is exposed to germs that cause disease, there is a delay in their creating the protective proteins (antibodies) needed to fight the infection.

While creating these antibodies, a pet can become very ill during this time and may be lost before they are able to fight the infection.

Also, infections may result in long-term negative effects.

In addition to preventing disease and loss of pets from disease, vaccinating lowers the cost of care of our pets. Diagnostic testing and treating pets that become ill is expensive and time-consuming, and it can be devastating for owners who love their pets.

Some canine (dog) vaccines owners may choose are:

D - distemper
H - canine infectious hepatitis
L - leptospirosis
P - parainfluenza (kennel cough)
P - parvo
C - corona virus
B - bordetella
RV - rabies vaccine
L - lyme

The first vaccine is a combination vaccine including the first five vaccines listed above and is referred to as the DHLPP vaccine. This vaccine is also known as:

- the Distemper/Parvo vaccine or
- the 5 in 1 vaccine.
- sometimes it is termed the 6 or 7 in 1 vaccine also, if additional vaccine parts (disease-causing agents) are included in the combination vaccine being used.

DISTEMPER

THE DHLPP:

D is for Distemper

The name *Distemper* is misleading—it is NOT a disease that causes a pet to become mean or ornery.

Distemper is caused by a virus—called a paramyxo virus (pair-ah-mix-oh) This information is included for you to dazzle your friends at parties.

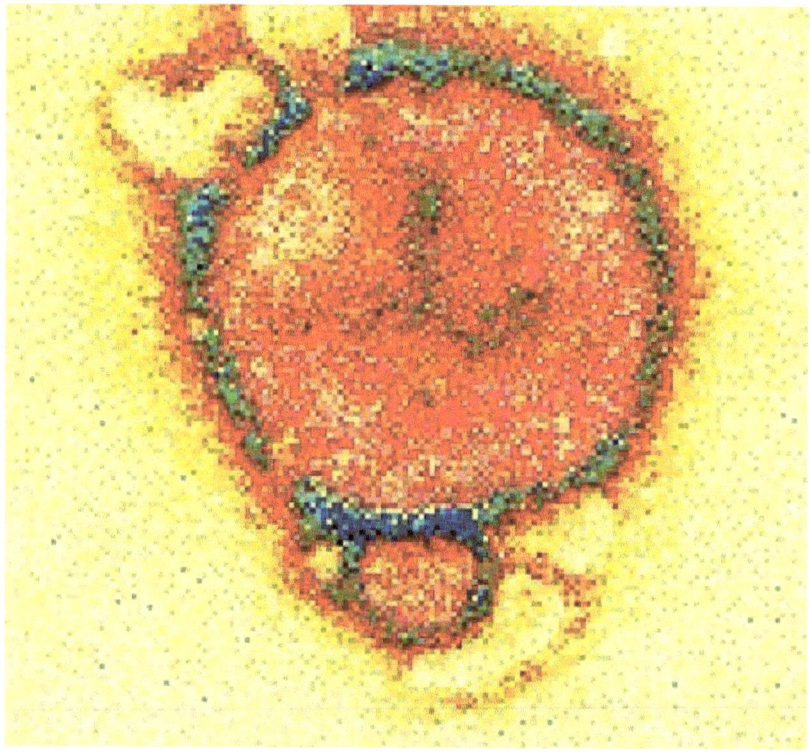

Canine Distemper virus magnified

Distemper is serious disease that may infect a dog's intestine, lungs, or brain.

Distemper is transferred from pet to pet by contact with saliva, feces, nasal or eye secretions, and infected urine. It can also be transferred in food and water. Wildlife like raccoons can also harbor this virus, as can wolves, foxes, and coyotes.

Dogs infected with distemper may show the following signs of illness:

1. there may not be signs of illness with mild infections
2. while there are lucky pets that survive infection with distemper, many do not
3. a dog may become depressed
4. a dog may stop eating
5. a dog may have diarrhea
6. a dog may vomit

More severely affected dogs can develop a high fever

1. they may have thick tan or white discharge from their eyes and nose
2. they may have difficulty breathing and cough
3. the most devastating symptoms occur if the distemper virus travels to the brain, causing seizures and mental disorders in the infected dog- when this happens it is unlikely the pet will survive

The GOOD NEWS is that the number one protection for your pet to prevent distemper is vaccination.

HEPATITIS

H is for Hepatitis

Canine Infectious Hepatitis is caused by a virus known as an adeno (add-en-oh) virus—type 1, to be more specific: CAV-1 (canine adeno virus type 1).

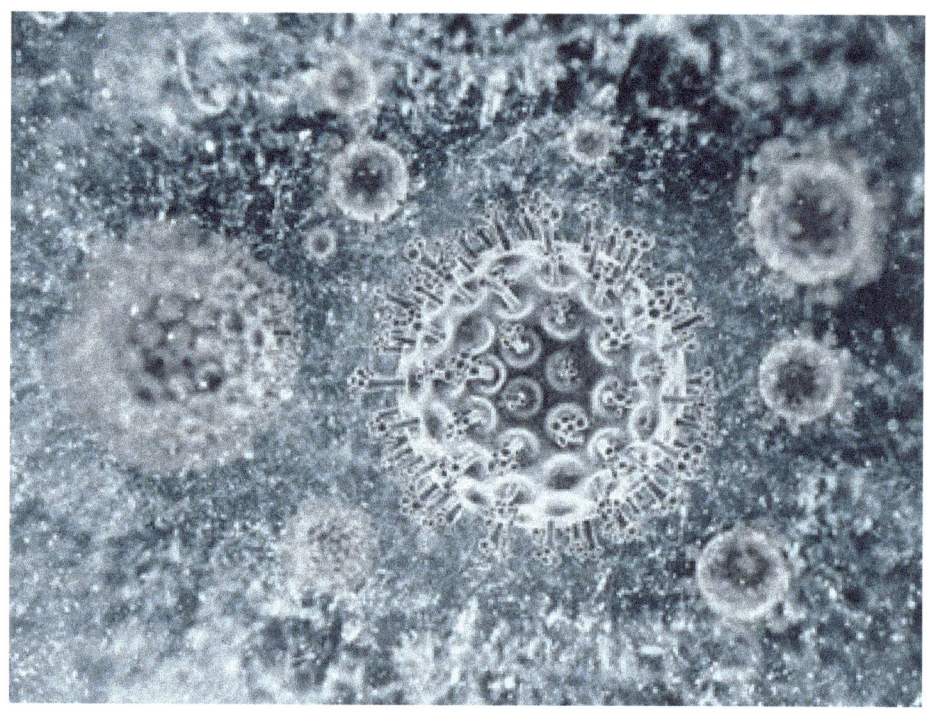

Canine Hepatitis virus magnified

Hepatitis is spread from pet to pet by contact with infected feces, urine, blood, saliva, and nasal discharge. Dogs may also be infected by wolves and coyotes. Hepatitis affects the liver and can also spread to the brain.

If a pet is infected with this virus, they may
1. be depressed
2. stop eating
3. cough
4. have a tender belly
5. have blood in their stool
6. become "yellow" (jaundiced) when the virus affects the liver
7. have bleeding that can cause bruising over the pet's body, or blood may be seen from the gums and in the stool and/or urine
8. have a change in the mental status of the pet occurs if the virus migrates to the brain— which is seen by owners as disorientation and confusion
9. and in some infections, the clear surface of the eyes—the cornea—becomes bluish colored

If a pet survives an infection with hepatitis, some of the symptoms listed above may not go away. Vaccinating is important for pets because this disease is eliminated or unnoticed when a pet is vaccinated.

LEPTOSPIROSIS

L is for Leptospirosis (lep-toe-spur-oh-sis). Lepto for short.

Leptospirosis is a serious bacterial disease affecting humans and animals. This bacteria is spiral shaped- like a corkscrew and found in the urine of infected animals.

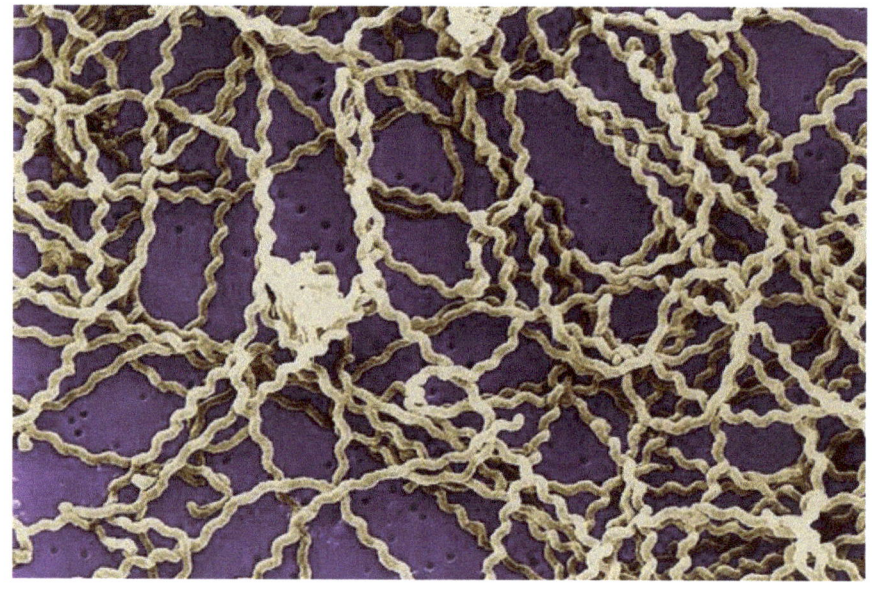

Leptospirosis bacteria magnified

Lepto bacteria can pass through a dog's mouth, eyes, or nose, but more importantly, it can penetrate the skin and spread throughout the body in the pet's blood. This is true for human infection also.

Infection can occur by animals or humans drinking contaminated water—even puddles on a road or in a field. Lepto bacteria can be found in the soil, water, and food contaminated with the urine of animals—such as cattle, pigs, horses, rodents, deer, and wildlife—infected with lepto.

Symptoms of Lepto include:
1. flu-like symptoms of not feeling well
2. decreased appetite
3. fever
4. depression
5. weakness
6. shivering
7. stiff muscles
8. vomiting and/or diarrhea that may or may not contain blood
9. symptoms may even include difficulty breathing, and cough
10. in more severe infections, pets become jaundiced (yellow colored in the gums, eyes, ears, belly skin) when the liver is involved
11. dogs drink more water if the bacteria infects the kidneys.
12. in severe infections, the kidneys are damaged and the dog may not make urine—this leads to loss of the pet

Although Lepto is more prevalent in wetter areas, all areas in the US and Canada are at risk.

All dogs are at risk.

Owners should always take care if working with water or urine potentially contaminated with Leptospirosis.

Wearing gloves and boots is helpful in protecting oneself.

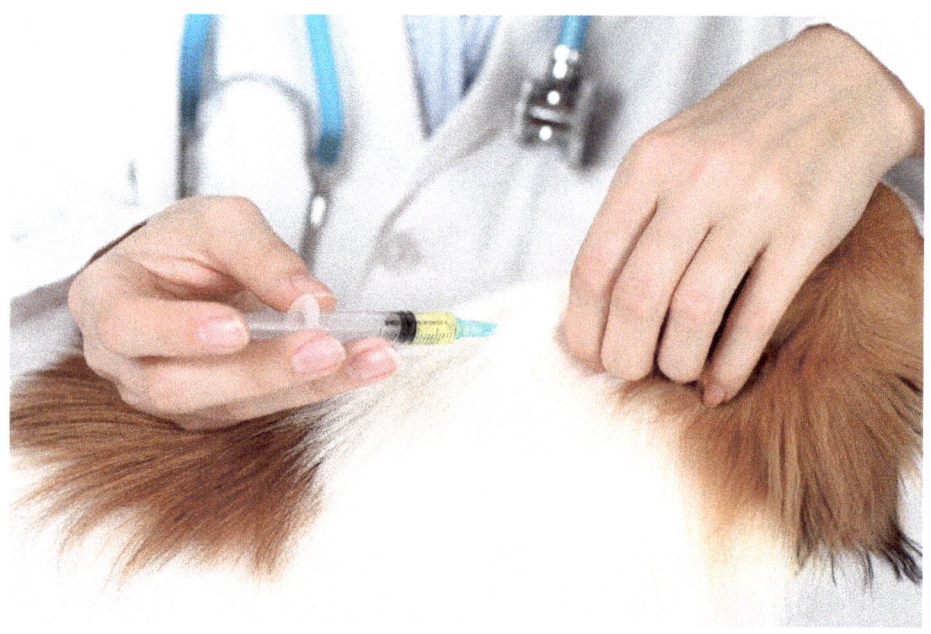

YES! Vaccine is available and is the best way to protect pets.

KENNEL COUGH (PARAINFLUENZA)

P is for Parainfluenza. (pair-ah-in- flu-en-zah).

Parainfluenza is caused by a virus resulting in a respiratory infection—a bronchitis.

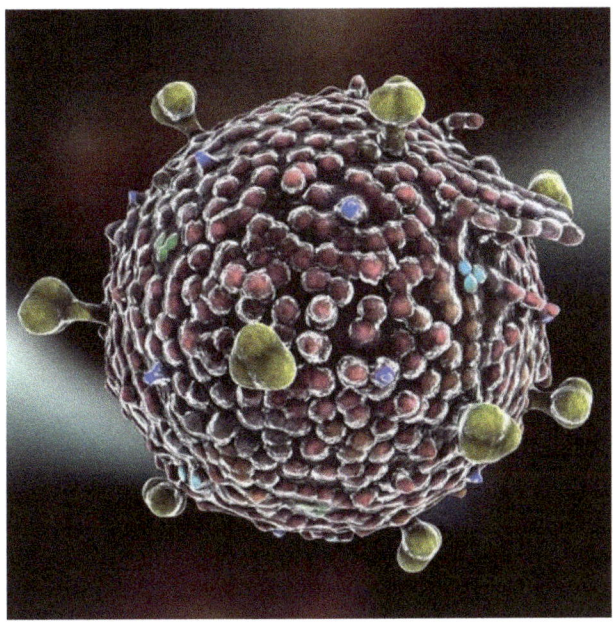

Parainfluenza virus magnified

Parainfluenza is a fancy word for a cold- or flu-like disease in dogs. It is also known as kennel cough, because pets kenneled together have a higher chance of spreading this to each other with breathing air in close quarters and barking—which spreads this airborne disease.

This virus is very contagious—which means dogs transfer it to other dogs very easily by contact or breathing the air of infected dogs.

Signs of parainfluenza include:
1. cough
2. fever
3. difficulty breathing
4. wheezing
5. sneezing
6. runny eyes
7. possibly conjunctivitis—infection around the eyes and eyelids
8. if left untreated, it may progress to pneumonia, with depression and lack of appetite—this may lead to the loss of a pet

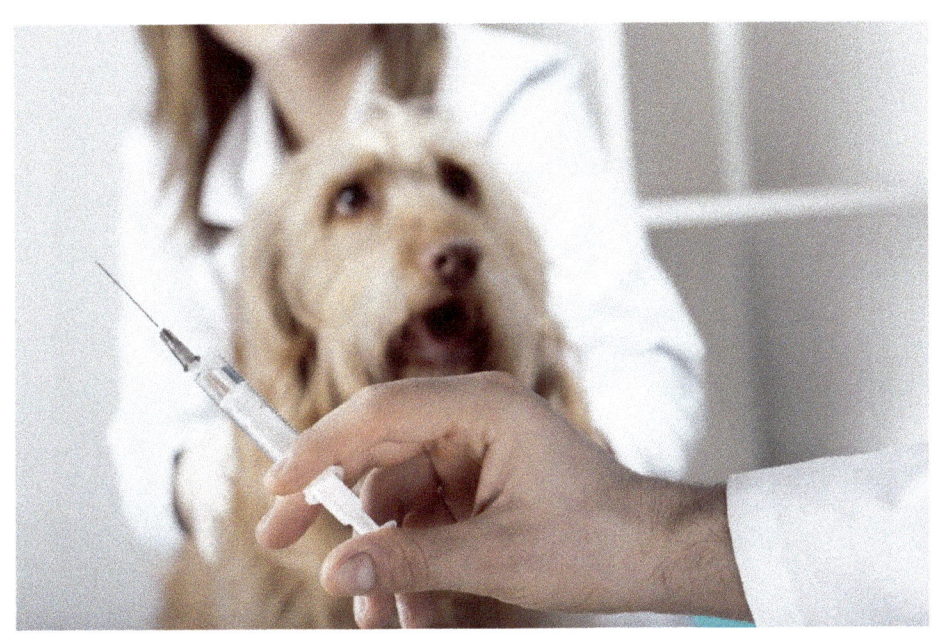

And… vaccination is the best method of protecting our dogs.

PARVO

P is also for Parvo (par-voh). Also known as Parvovirus.

Parvo is caused by a virus that attacks the lining of the intestines.

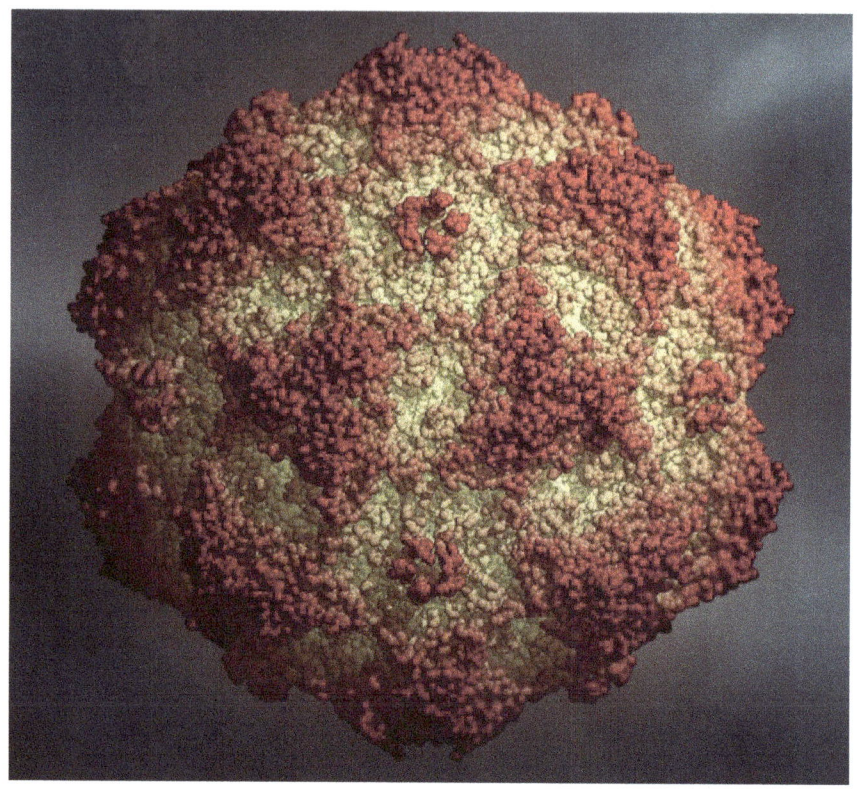

Parvovirus magnified

Parvo is spread from pet to pet by direct contact. It can also be spread on clothing or shoes of humans in close contact with a dog infected with parvo virus.

When the parvo virus attacks and irritates the lining of the intestines, it causes:

1. diarrhea that often has blood present
2. vomiting
3. loss of appetite
4. depression
5. dehydration results from fluid loss from vomiting, diarrhea, and not drinking
6. another serious concern in parvo infection is that the virus attacks a dog's white blood cells (cells that protect dogs from infection) - when a decrease in white blood cells happens, this makes him/her susceptible to life-threatening infections such as pneumonia

Treatment for parvo is costly and includes vigorous administration of intravenous fluids, antibiotics, and other medications. Treatment may be necessary for 2–10 days depending on how a dog's body responds to the virus and treatment.

Young puppies infected with parvo virus may have heart damage if the virus infects the heart. When this occurs, even if the pup survives the parvo infection, damage to the heart will not heal or improve. This may be a reason for loss of a pup from parvovirus.

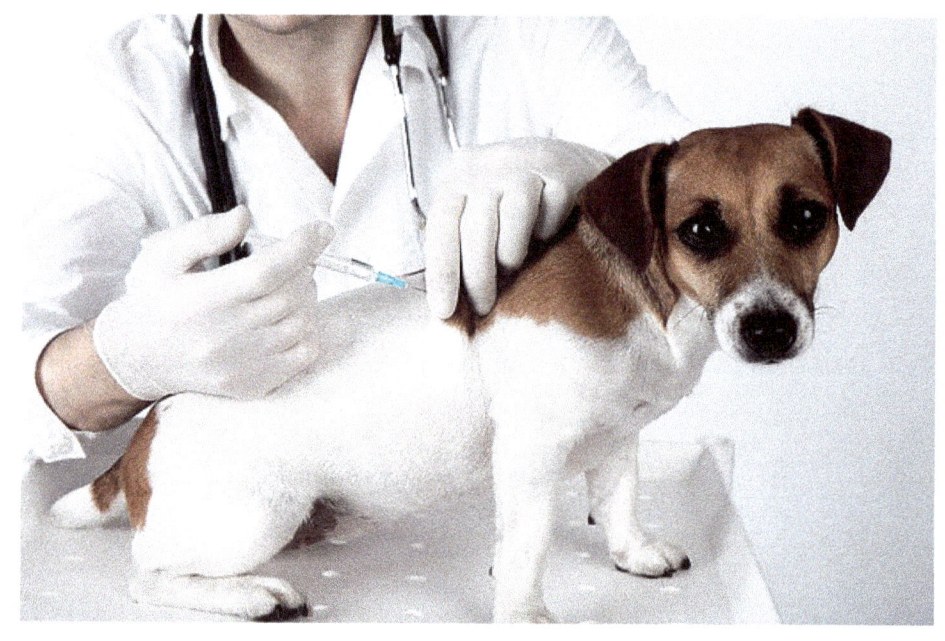

YES! The best prevention of parvo virus infection is vaccination.

CORONA VIRUS

Corona (kah-row-nah) virus

Coronavirus is named because it is a virus that is shaped like a crown—corona means crown.

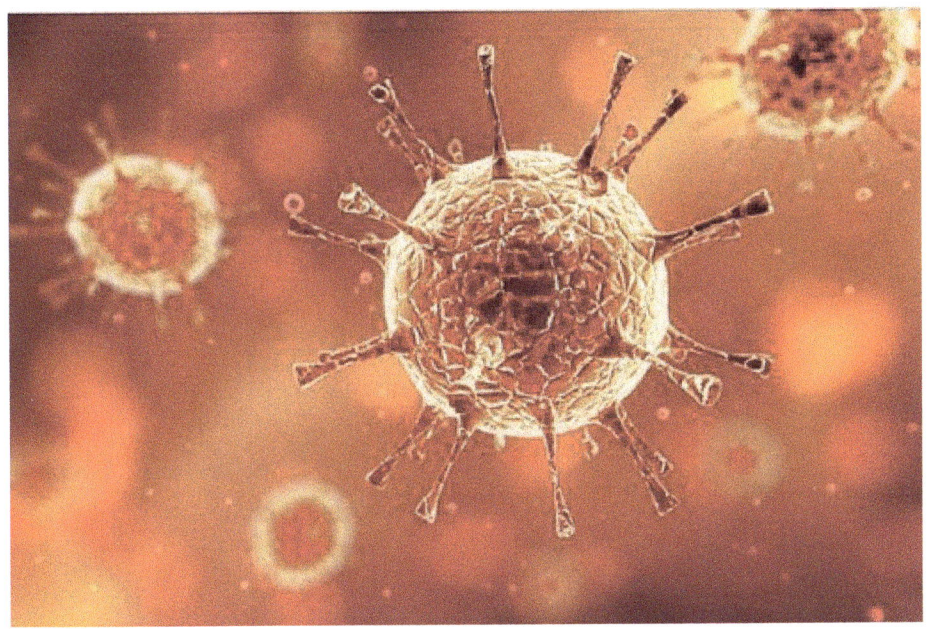

Coronavirus magnified

Corona virus is spread from pet to pet by contact with feces that is infected with the virus.

Corona virus infection is similar to parvo virus in that it is an intestinal virus, but milder. However, if it occurs along with parvo virus infection, the corona viral infection can be more complicated and severe.

Signs of infection with corona virus include:

1. dehydration that is less severe than parvo virus, but still serious; as well as diarrhea that may or may not have blood present
2. vomiting
3. loss of appetite
4. depression

Treatment for corona virus infection includes fluids and antibiotics, medication for vomiting and diarrhea, antibiotics, and a bland diet. Most pets recover from corona virus; however, some do not.

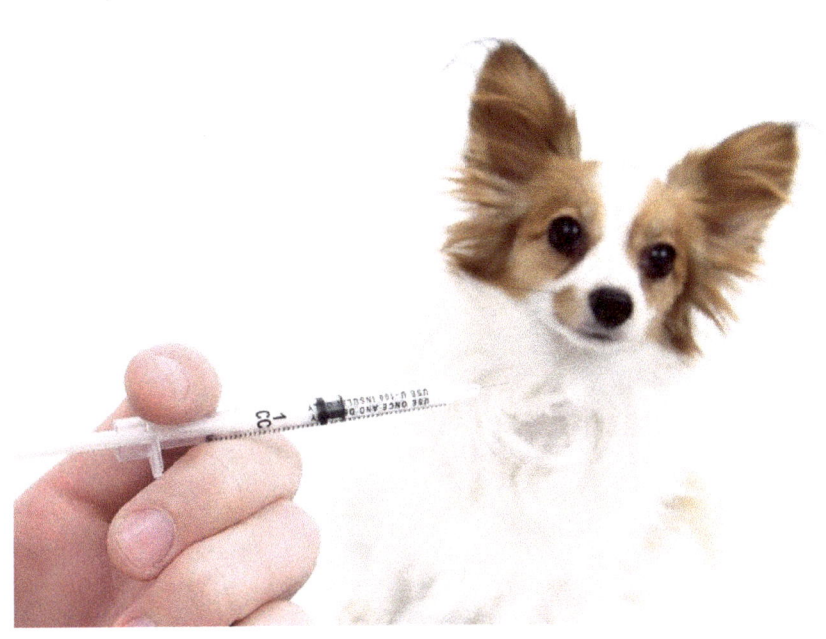

Vaccine is available and usually recommended for puppies to avoid the illness, expensive treatment, and potential pet loss. Corona virus vaccine may be a separate vaccine or added to the DHLPP, making it a DHLPP-C.

BORDETELLA

Bordetella is a respiratory infection also known as kennel cough (tracheobronchitis) in dogs.

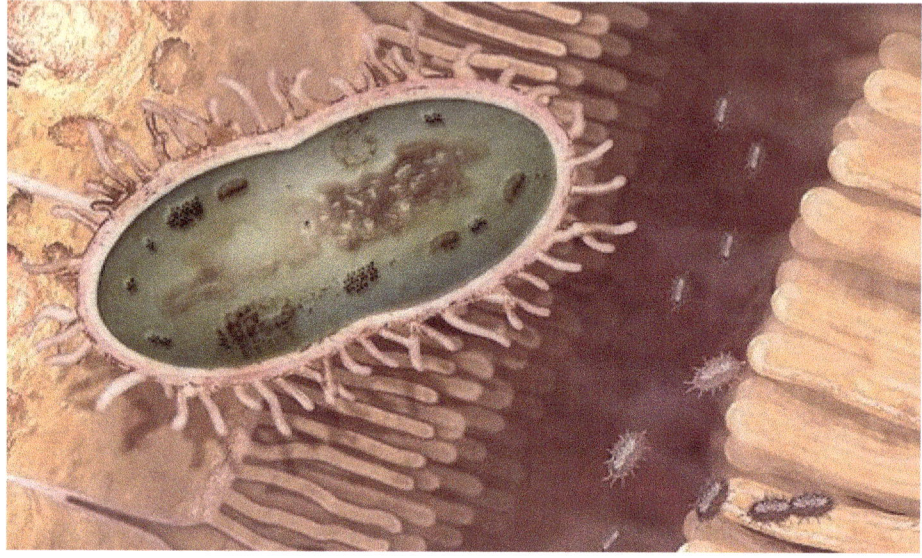

Bordetella magnified

Bordetella is transferred from pet to pet by direct contact with respiratory droplets that contain the bordetella bacteria in the air.

Signs of kennel cough include:
1. a dry hacking cough
2. cough with white, tan, yellow or other colored sputum
3. nasal discharge that is clear, white, tan, yellow or green
4. fever
5. depression
6. difficulty breathing

Puppies are more susceptible to infection and if untreated, may progress to pneumonia and even loss of the pet.

Treatment is essential. Antibiotics and cough suppressants are recommended.

As always, vaccinating and keeping puppies away from other dogs until sufficiently vaccinated is the best approach to preventing kennel cough from bordetella.

Bordetella vaccine can be given as an injection (shot), as an oral (by mouth) vaccine, or with nasal drops.

There may controversy about this vaccine; however, this author has seen effective prevention of kennel cough with the use of this vaccine.

RABIES

Rabies is a serious and devastating disease of warm-blooded animals—including humans—that is caused by a virus called a rhabdo (rabb-doe) virus. There is no cure for rabies in pets.

Rabies virus magnified

Rabies is transmitted between warm-blooded animals by bites or exposure to the saliva of an animal that has rabies. These warm-blooded animals include other dogs, cats, raccoons, skunks, foxes, bats, and even horses and cattle. Essentially any warm-blooded animal can contract rabies.

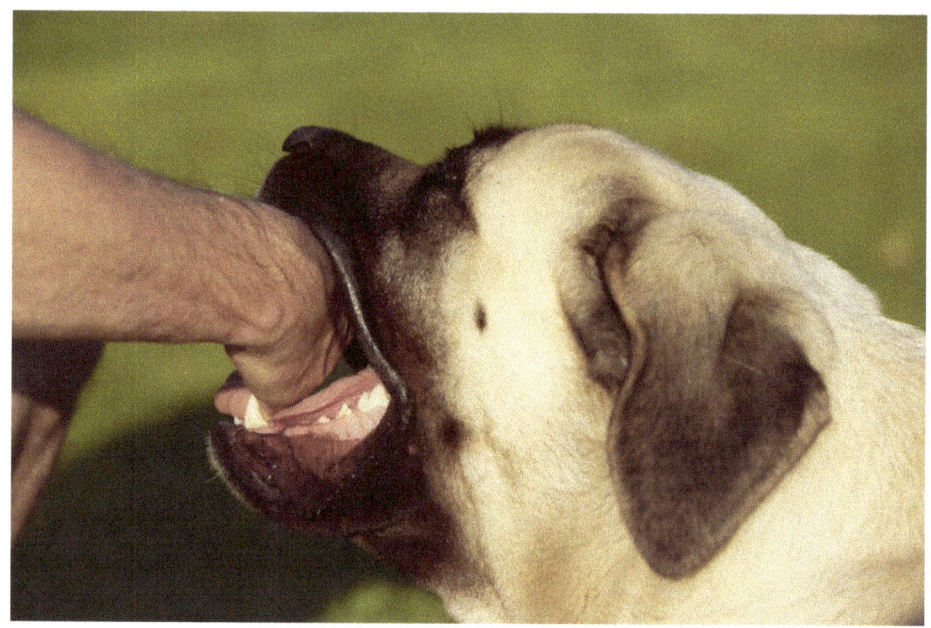

An important consideration with rabies is that humans can contract rabies from the bite of an infected animal or exposure to an infected animal's saliva.

The signs of rabies vary. Two forms of rabies are described:

MAD FORM
salivating
angry—acting "mad"
biting even if usually not a biter

DUMB FORM
quiet
appears dazed
change in personality

Since there is no treatment for rabies, health departments and governments around the country recommend and may require vaccinating all eligible animals for rabies. As noted, rabies is a disease that may affect humans.

LYME DISEASE

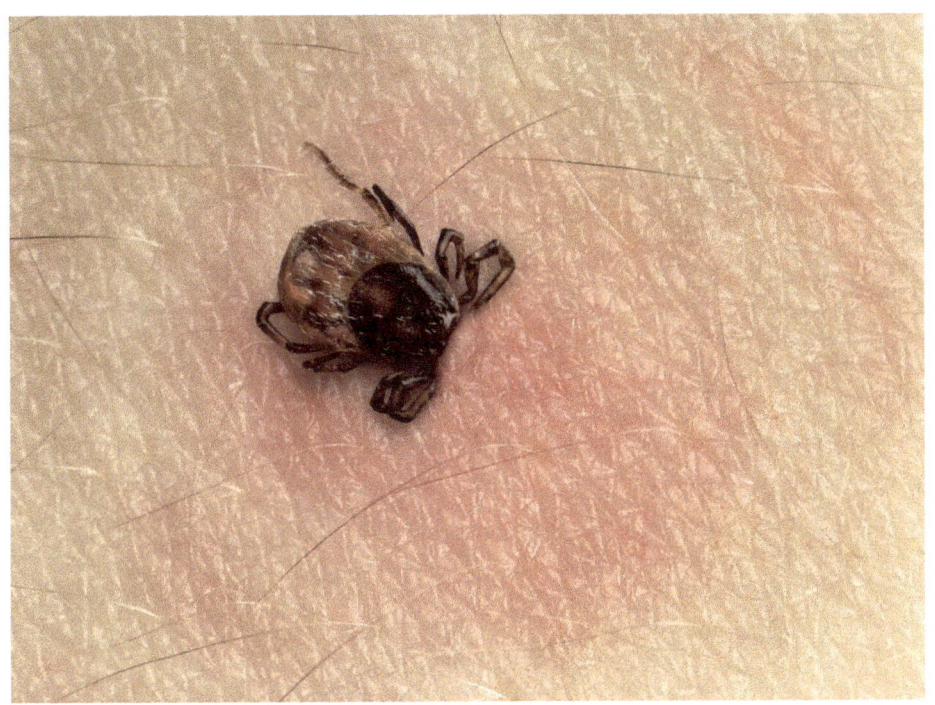

Lyme is caused by a bacteria shaped like a spring (a spirochete) of the Borrelia species. Lyme is transferred to dogs or humans by ticks.

Dogs do not give their owners Lyme disease; however, the ticks that can attach to dogs can attach to humans and cause Lyme disease.

The symptoms of Lyme disease may vary from:
1. no symptoms
2. just not feeling well
3. not eating
4. vomiting
5. more serious symptoms include joint irritation with swelling and pain to the pet's joints
6. joint involvement leads to the pet shifting weight from one leg to another while walking or standing
7. when experiencing difficulty walking, a pet may also appear stiff, arch their back, or have difficulty breathing
8. when Lyme disease becomes more serious, a pet's heart or kidneys may be damaged and kidney failure may occur
9. also, if Lyme affects the nervous areas of the pet, this may lead to weakness or a change in a dog's behavior

When symptoms of Lyme disease occur, several weeks of antibiotics may be required to treat this disease.

Goals for preventing Lyme disease include:

- vaccinate for Lyme disease in high-incidence areas
- prevent ticks from attaching—there are many products available for dogs
- remove any ticks as soon as possible
- the longer a tick is attached, the more chance there is of a disease occurring
- treat any indication of a disease early

IMPORTANT: The longer a tick is on a pet, the greater chance for the tick to transmit a disease.

Some dogs infected with Lyme disease have successfully made their own protection and do not show symptoms of Lyme. This exposure or infection may be detected on tests for Lyme disease.

Ticks range in size from large to so tiny they are difficult to see. Search pets closely for any ticks and use tick products if you are in high-tick area.

Vaccinating is recommended.

Talk to your veterinarian about vaccine recommendations and schedules.

SPECIAL NEEDS FOR PUPPIES

Puppies receive a series of vaccinations because when pups are born, they receive the protective proteins (antibodies) while drinking their mothers' milk.

These protective proteins are called "maternal" (mother) antibodies. These maternal antibodies protect young pups from the diseases that affect dogs; however, they do not last more than 14–16 weeks.

Mothers' antibodies interfere with a pup making its own protection. Knowing this, veterinarians administer a series of vaccines which are given every 2–4 weeks until the pup is 14–16 weeks old—when mom's protection is gone and it is certain a pup has made their own protective antibodies.

It is not as important to consider WHEN a pup's vaccines are begun as much as WHEN they are completed, to insure adequate protection for one year. Check with your veterinarian for their recommendations.

Yes, vaccines prevent disease or lessen the severity of disease. They lower the cost of care for pets.

Most of the time one cannot even tell a pet has received a vaccine; however…

…..adverse reactions to vaccines can occur. These reactions are uncommon; however, they can be alarming and even devastating.

ADVERSE REACTIONS TO VACCINES

Reactions range from mild soreness at the injection site to not playing or eating/drinking as well for 1–2 days after being vaccinated.

More severe reactions include:

- swelling to a pet's face
- diarrhea and/or vomiting
- fever
- hives or any rash on the dog's skin

Severity of signs may progress to anaphylaxis, which includes:
- difficulty breathing
- lower blood pressure—may be noticed by the pet staggering and unable to walk
- seizures
- shock
- coma
- loss of pet

All adverse signs/symptoms noted by owners should be taken seriously and reported to their veterinarian; however, the more severe symptoms need treatment by a veterinarian in an office or emergency clinic.

Reactions can be frightening to owners and may discourage vaccinating. If a pet has experienced an adverse reaction to a vaccine, or an owner would like to prevent reactions in high-risk pets, veterinarians may recommend pre-treating pets prior to vaccinating to reduce or eliminate the risk of an adverse reaction from occurring.

Chapter 4
TICK DISEASES

Ticks are not to be taken lightly. If you or your dogs have been bitten by a tick, your dog may be affected with:

(Important Facts about Ticks)

An important fact about ticks is that the diseases they can cause in pets, they can also cause in humans.

As a pet owner, it is advisable to know what ticks are common in the area you live and what diseases they transmit.

Unlike Lyme disease, there are no vaccines for the 6 additional tick diseases addressed in this chapter.

The goals regarding ticks and preventing disease are:

- prevent ticks from attaching—there are many products available for dogs
- remove any ticks as soon as possible- the longer a tick is attached, the more chance there is of a disease occurring
- treat any indication of disease early
- take care that you do not allow ticks to attach to you

Ehrlichiosis (ur-lick-ee-oh-sis)

Transmitted by the Brown Dog Tick and the Lone Star Tick

Ehrlichiosis is seen mostly in the SW and Gulf regions of the USA, however, this disease has been noted in dogs from Tennessee, Kentucky, and Florida as well.

Lone Star Tick

Signs of Ehrlichiosis include:
1. depression
2. loss of appetite
3. discharge from the nose and eyes that may be clear or cloudy white, tan, yellow
4. spontaneous bleeding from the nose and mouth may be seen, along with bruising anywhere on an infected pet's body.
5. infected dogs may experience joint pain, and the pet may not be able to walk well.

And remember, ticks can be very small and difficult to find.

Ehrlichiosis can be transmitted to humans.

Anaplasmosis (an-uh-plaz-moh-sis)

Anaplasmosis (an-uh-plaz-moh-sis) is a tick-borne disease that can affect many animals, including the dog.

Transmitted by the Deer Tick, Brown Dog Ticks, and ticks that also carry Lyme disease.

Signs of Anaplasmosis include:

- joint pain and stiffness
- fever
- listlessness
- loss of appetite
- vomiting
- diarrhea
- infrequently, seizures may be seen.

Brown Dog Tick

Rocky Mountain Spotted Fever (RMSF)

Rocky Mountain spotted fever is a common tick-borne disease that affects dogs and humans. It is caused by *Rickettsia rickettsii* (the organism responsible for Rocky Mountain spotted fever)—which lives parasitically in ticks and is transmitted by bite to animals and humans.

RMSF is transmitted by the American Dog Tick, the Lone Star Tick, the Brown Dog Tick, and several other ticks.

Rocky Mountain spotted fever tick

RMSF may be seen anywhere in the US; however, the highest number of infections are seen in the 8 Rocky Mountain States and in California and South Eastern States.

RMSF may have mild or no symptoms, so an owner may not be aware an infection has happened. These lucky dogs usually recover quickly and completely.

A more severe form of RMSF can occur with many different symptoms developing 2–14 days after being bitten by a tick. Symptoms may include:
- depression
- decreased appetite
- listlessness
- fever
- blood in the urine
- irregular heart beat (arrhythmia)
- discolored spots along the skin, often bruised or purplish in color; sometimes little spots of bruising scattered over the pet's body
- inability to walk normally, loss of coordination (ataxia)
- swelling or edema (fluid retention) to the face or legs
- bleeding that occurs suddenly, most often from the nose, or in the stools
- bleeding from the pet's eyes
- difficulty clotting blood (stopping bleeding), which can lead to shock or death
- swollen lymph nodes
- pain in the eyes
- pneumonia
- vomiting and diarrhea
- pain and/or swelling in the joints
- or other symptoms

Testing for Rocky Mountain Spotted Fever

Testing for Rocky Mountain Spotted fever includes

- blood tests for "titers"—the measure of the protective proteins (antibodies) created by an infected pet against RMSF
- a biopsy can also help test for RMSF—this is a procedure in which a small skin sample is taken and sent to specialists who examine the skin under the microscope to determine if a disorder is present

If a pet is ill with RMSF, immediate treatment is necessary. Do not hesitate to have pets who have had ticks on them seen by a veterinarian.

Hepatozoonosis (hep-at-oh-zo-in-oh-sis)

Transmitted by the Gulf Coast Tick and the Brown Dog Tick

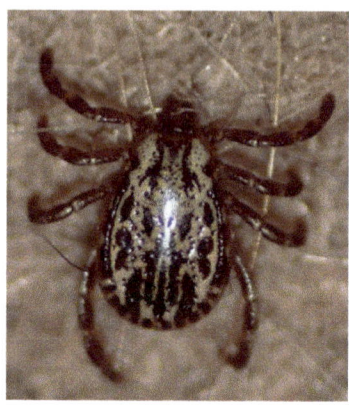

Gulf Coast Tick

Unlike the other tick diseases, Hepatozoonosis is not acquired by pets from being bitten by the tick. They acquire this disorder when they ingest (eat) the tick while grooming themselves or chewing at themselves due to the irritation from the tick attachment.

Hepatozoonosis is most often seen in the Eastern and Mid-Southern USA.

Signs of Hepatozoonosis include:
1. weight loss
2. decreased appetite
3. depression
4. fever
5. eye irritation
6. pain all over the pet's body
7. this disease may affect the muscles of the pet, resulting in debilitation and an inability to walk, or a decrease in the size of a dog's muscles.

Also, Hepatozoonosis may result in the loss of the pet.

Babesiosis (baa-bee-zee-oh-sis)

Transmitted by the Brown Dog Tick; also, dogs can infect each other through biting one another.

Signs of Babesiosis include:
1. anemia—low number of red blood cells
2. pale color to the gums above the pet's teeth as well as inside the ears from anemia
3. weakness
4. decreased appetite
5. vomiting
6. weight loss

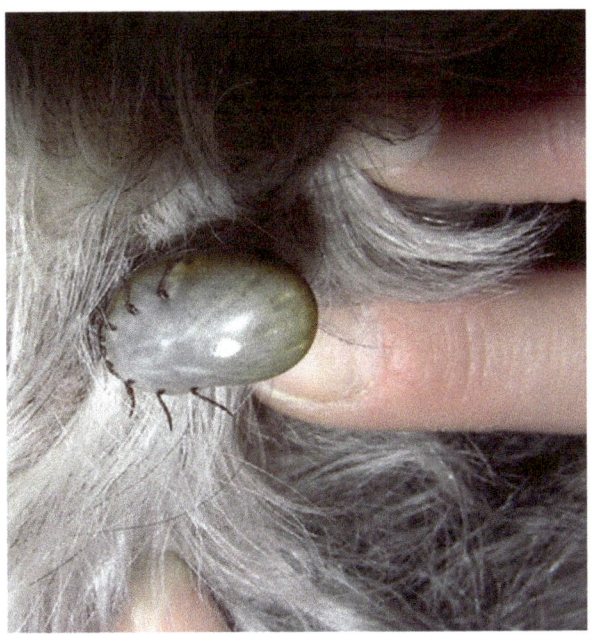

a gorged Brown Dog Tick

TICK PARALYSIS

As this syndrome describes, some ticks render dogs suddenly unable to walk. If you see a tick on your pet and he is not able to walk, remove the tick immediately and seek veterinary care.

Tick Paralysis Tick

TICK REMOVAL

There are effective medications available to prevent ticks and tick-borne diseases. These tick medications are available through your veterinarian and are recommended if your pet is in a high-tick-infested area.

Also, it is important to remove ticks immediately—the longer a tick is attached the more chance a tick disease can be transmitted to a dog.

Treatment is available for any dogs that show signs of tick diseases. Seek veterinarian care.

Removal of ticks is simple:

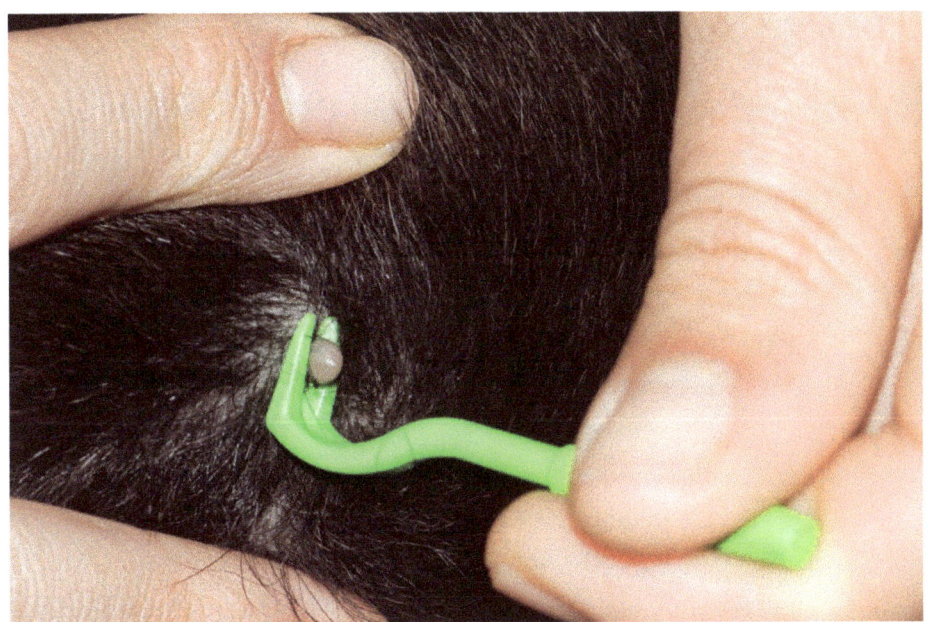

1. have help to hold the dog still
2. WEAR GLOVES because humans can get diseases from ticks and their body fluids

3. if available, pour a small amount of 70% isopropyl alcohol near the head attachment of the tick
4. using tweezers, or special instruments made to remove ticks, hold the tweezers sideways and grab the tick as close to the skin of the dog as possible
5. pull straight up to remove the tick
6. DO NOT twist or jerk the tick—this may lead to leaving mouth parts in the skin
7. if mouth parts have not been removed completely, use a warm compress to the area
8. DO NOT squeeze the tick or crush the body of the tick—because its fluids (saliva and guts contents) may contain organisms that can infect the dog

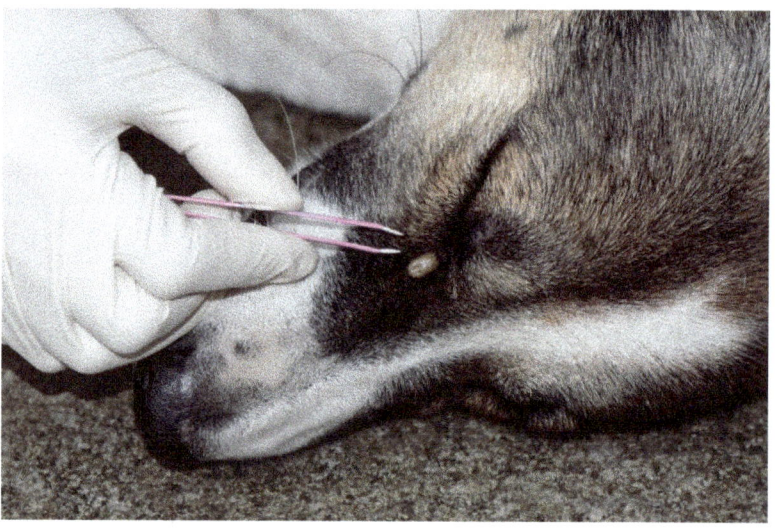

9. seek veterinary care as soon as possible to examine the pet and the tick attachment site
10. have the pet tested for tick diseases after a tick attachment—especially if ill
11. if necessary use medication for tick diseases
12. do not throw in the garbage or down the toilet—this does not kill a tick—a jar is recommended

Chapter 5
SPAYING AND NEUTERING

SPAY – a surgical procedure to remove the ovaries and uterus of the female dog.

This procedure is also known as an Ovario Hysterectomy (OHE).

NEUTER – also called castration – a surgical procedure to remove the testicles of the male dog.

SPAY AND NEUTER ARE THE LOVING CHOICE

Good for your dog

REASONS TO SPAY

- no puppies
- no "heat" cycles and messy discharges
- decrease incidence of mammary gland tumors
- no chance of pyometra (life-threatening infection in the uterus)
- pets live longer

REASONS TO NEUTER

- no puppies
- less prostate disorders
- less chance of male behavior (urine-marking, roaming, humping, fighting)
- decreased incidence of perianal growths
- decreased incidence of perianal hernias
- pets live longer

Good for you

- no stress of heat (estrous) cycles
- no unwanted puppies
- no stress of pets running loose—possibly being injured or lost
- less cost for surgeries that are uncomplicated

Good for the community

- saves millions of dollars spent controlling unwanted animals
- decreases pressure on animal shelters to house or euthanize animals
- decreases number of stray and homeless animals—a homeless life is a sad and dangerous life for pets—filled with hunger, disease, exposure to the weather, and being uncared for
- decreases the diseases in the stray population that threaten owned pets with disease and injury

Spaying and neutering prices vary depending on locations where these procedures are completed.

If prices quoted are more than expected, there are low-cost centers that may be considered.

WHEN TO SPAY AND NEUTER

When should you spay or neuter?

It is this author's understanding it is best to spay a female dog prior to any cycle or as soon as possible to decrease the potential complications included in this chapter for pets not spayed. Early neutering also prevents disorders listed in this chapter.

Most privately practicing veterinary clinics recommend spaying/neutering between 5 1/2 and 6 months. Some clinics charge higher costs for older or overweight pets because procedures on these pets can be more difficult, take more time, and have more risk to the procedure.

Some animal shelters complete spays and neuters on all dogs to decrease the unwanted pet population. Some spays and neuters are on very young pets before they are adopted.

COMPLICATIONS OF SPAYING AND NEUTERING

Despite all the very good reasons to spay and neuter our pets, sometimes complications occur.

Uncommon complications may include:

- cost
- anesthetic risks
- infection
- pets removing their sutures, requiring additional surgery and experiencing delays in healing
- inside sutures loosening, requiring additional care
- small pieces of ovaries remaining, resulting in symptoms of heat cycles and other possible complications

WAYS TO MINIMIZE COMPLICATIONS OF SPAYING AND NEUTERING

Knowing there may be risks frightens some owners; however, as stated, there are many risks when a pet is not spayed or neutered that could be devastating to pets and owners. As with all situations, benefits outweigh risks.

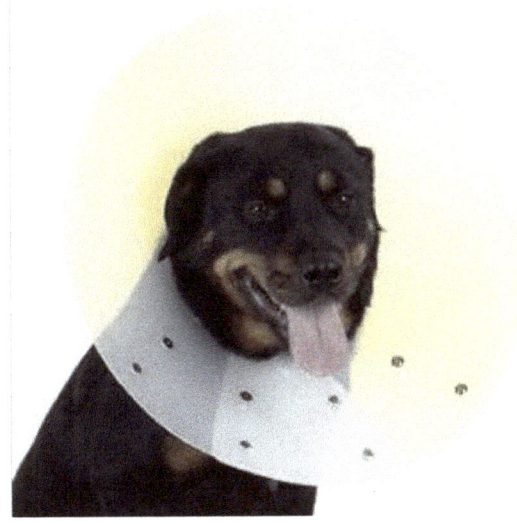

To minimize spay/neuter complications:
- have surgery completed on young pets
- do not allow your pet to become overweight before spaying/neutering
- schedule the surgery when someone can watch the pet for several days after surgery
- purchase an Elizabethan collar (AKA an e-collar or lampshade) and place it on the pet to prevent them chewing stitches from surgical sites, or licking—which can lead to opening of surgical incision and can cause infection

Chapter 6

WHAT TO EXPECT WHEN YOUR DOG IS EXPECTING

For owners who want to have puppies or owners who did not read chapter 5!

GETTING PREGNANT

FIRST THINGS FIRST... GETTING PREGNANT

- estrous (heat) cycles begin in female dogs at 6–10 months of age- heat cycles occur about every 6–10 months after their first heat cycle, depending on the dog
- visible signs of "heat" may last 5–21 days
- as a general rule, red discharge is seen first, then pinkish, then whitish discharge
- dogs are more likely to become pregnant during the "heat" cycle when the red discharge is seen
- male dogs may be able to make puppies between 6 and 12 months of age, however, most are able between 6 and 8 months of age
- females should be bred with the male dog every other day while showing signs of heat and receptiveness to the male
- if necessary, testing is available to predict when a female dog is ready to become pregnant -testing cells from the vaginal tract or blood testing of hormone levels may be recommended -always discuss options with your veterinarian
- pregnancy lasts approximately 63 days
- when a female dog is not pregnant, non-visible heat may continue for 60–100 days after the visible signs begin- signs of false pregnancy may occur and include weight gain, mammary development, and milk production due to high levels of hormones -dogs showing signs of false pregnancy may carry toys or nest as if they are going to have pups, but do not

Most female dogs have no difficulty becoming pregnant; however, when nature is not taking its course, veterinarians may recommend:

- artificial insemination—in which the veterinarian collects semen from the male dog into a container, then instills the semen into the female dog with a catheter
- surgical insemination—which includes placing the female dog under anesthesia, opening her abdomen, identifying the uterus, and instilling semen directly into the uterus with a needle and syringe

YES! We're pregnant!

- nutritional needs of pregnant dogs increase when pregnant and increase more as pregnancy continues and after the pups are born
- pregnant and mommy dogs need access to food and water at all times
- as the mother dog provides milk for the pups, she gives them nutrition from her body -as the pups grow, they require more nutrition from her - pups take the most nutrition from their mother when they are 5 weeks of age—close to the time of weaning
- this is why mother dogs need the most nutrition for themselves and the pups by the time the pups are 5 weeks of age—especially if there is a large number of puppies
- mom may become very thin if she is not given enough food and water
- it is recommended to feed a high-calorie food free choice during these periods of care for a pregnant dog -ask your veterinarian for their recommendations
- often nursing moms will lose hair during the time they are taking care of the pups

BENEFITS OF X-RAYS WHEN PREGNANT

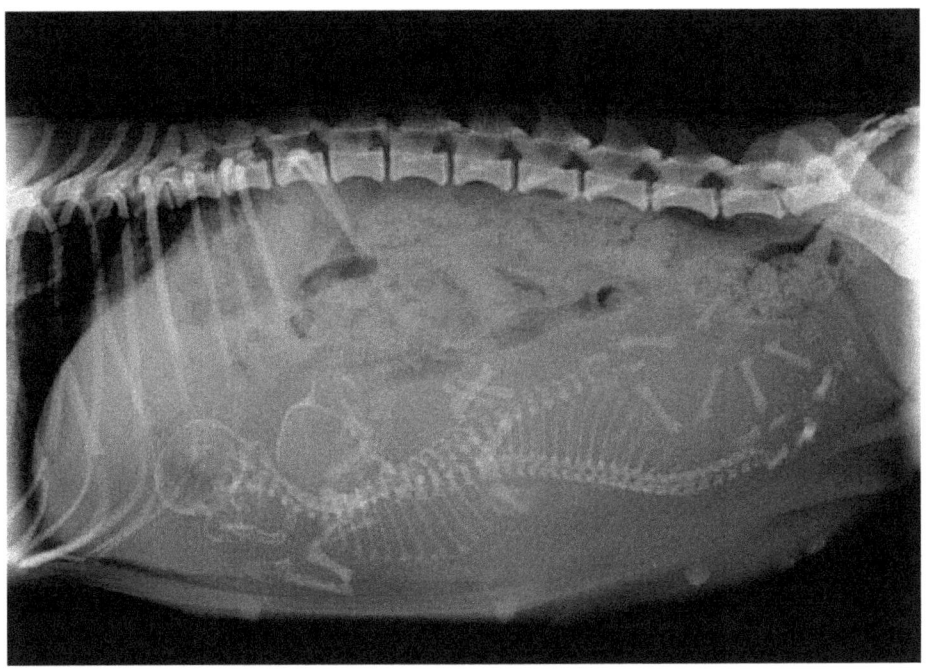

The skeletons of unborn pups cannot be seen on x-rays until after 42 days of pregnancy (remember the pregnancy lasts 63 days).

X-rays are beneficial because they can:
1. help make sure the pups are healthy
2. help determine the number of pups so everyone will know how many pups to expect
3. help determine when all the pups have been born-if she is not able to deliver all the pups, care can be sought quickly.
4. help determine the size of the pups-if they are too big, the mother may need a cesarean-section—a surgery to deliver the pups.

Ultrasound can be completed early in pregnancy to count puppies and visualize heart beats of puppies.

The motto of pup delivery is: "Leave no pup behind!"

BEING PREPARED

When it comes close to the time for the pups to be born (whelping the pups), it is important to be prepared.

Helpful supplies are:
1. a whelping area—preferably a box large enough for the mother dog to be able to move around in with the puppies
2. a quiet place to have the puppies
3. a bulb syringe for the pups if needed for fluids in the pups' mouths and noses
4. clean dry towels
5. reading material to learn about the puppy delivery process, to know what to expect
6. being prepared to stay with a new mother while she is delivering and afterward as well
7. knowledge that it may take as short as 2–3 hours to have the pups and as long as 24
8. scissors to clip any long hair around the milk glands (the mammary glands) so the pups can nurse easily
9. a calendar to help calculate the 63 days "due" to deliver.
10. emergency numbers handy along with the locations of local clinics and emergency clinic prior to having the pups

STAGE 1 OF PUPPY DELIVERY

The dog…

- may become restless and begin trying to find a quiet safe place to have the pups
- may stop eating
- may try to stay very close to her owner
- may begin to lick at her vulva
- will begin to have a clear or cloudy mucous from her vulva

ADDITIONALLY: when mother dogs begin to become restless and make "nests" for the pups, they want to be secluded or they may worry and harm the pups because they are frightened they cannot protect them.

The owner…

- should set aside a private, quiet space with a whelping box for the mom
- should have only 1 or 2 people around the mom and pups during delivery
- should stay with her and observe her—the way she is acting and the way she treats her pups

STAGE 2 OF PUPPY DELIVERY

The dog…
- may begin digging in her box to nest
- may begin licking her vulva more than the first stage
- may shiver
- may become more restless than the first stage

The owner…
- should stay with the mom
- should have all the supplies close and ready to use
- should be prepared

STAGE 3 OF PUPPY DELIVERY

The dog:

- she should begin having her puppies
- a water sac should be visible at the opening of the vulva
- the mother may pant, grunt, and push a puppy out
- normal time to push is 2–10 minutes when the pup is in the birth canal
- the mother should remove the sac that surrounds the pup, begin licking the pup to stimulate breathing, and dry the pup (if she does not, see the "owner" section next)
- most pups are delivered head first, some are delivered back legs first—as long as the pup is able to pass, both deliveries are normal
- a placenta may follow each pup or be delivered later
- green and black discharge is normal AFTER a puppy has been delivered—it is never normal before puppies have been delivered
- be prepared for a large amount of fluid to soil towels, blankets, and the whelping box during delivery—which need to be removed and replaced with dry ones after delivery—and sometimes after several pups in large litters

The owner:

- observe the delivery of each pup
- make sure the mother is caring for the pups
- observe the mother for signs of confusion about the new pups and help as needed—even if this means removing the pups to protect them
- make sure mom does not accidentally hurt the pups because she is confused
- make sure the umbilical cord is tied off with floss or clean thread if the mother has not done so—tie off 1/4–1/2 inch from the pup's belly when tying off the cord before cutting the cord from the placenta
- if the sac is not removed by the mother dog, remove it from the pup
- after the sac has been removed, clean and dry the face and nostrils of the puppy if the mother is not cleaning and drying the pup (some owners use a bulb syringe to remove fluid from the nose and mouths of pups)
- gently massage the pup with a warm, dry towel until it is dry
- try to avoid allowing the mother dog to eat the afterbirths—these may make her vomit

WHEN TO WORRY

While most deliveries go off without a hitch, there are times an owner should be concerned and seek medical attention.

Seek help immediately if your whelping mom begins to:

1. push without producing a puppy within 30 minutes
2. have blood coming from her vulva
3. become exhausted
4. collapse
5. become unresponsive to you
6. have a pup come, but not be able to be delivered from the birth canal and you are unable to gently remove the pup yourself
7. stop delivering puppies for 2 hours when you know more puppies need to come
8. have two puppies trying to be delivered at one time
9. cry and appear in pain
10. appear depressed
11. concern you for any reason

WHAT TO DO

In the event that the birth of the pups needs medical care, a C-section (cesarean section) may be necessary.

C-section is a surgical procedure in which an incision is made to open the abdomen, and another incision is made to open the uterus so the puppies may be removed with the surgeon's hands.

A C-section should be performed by a veterinarian as soon as it is determined the mother dog is unable to deliver the puppies herself. Sometimes c-sections are scheduled for dogs known to have delivery difficulty, such as bulldogs.

A delay in seeking medical care may cause loss of the puppies and possibly the mother dog.

THE PUPPIES ARE HERE

After mom has her pups:

    1. make sure the mother makes milk -the first milk will appear slightly yellowish and is called colostrum - it is this early milk that has protection for the diseases discussed in earlier chapters

    2. in a few days, the milk will turn white and should never have an odor

    3. examine the mother's mammary glands (the milk glands) daily to make sure they are soft and filled with milk

    4. if the mammary glands become firm, hot, red, swollen, bumpy, or have anything but white milk coming from them, the mother dog needs medical care immediately

    5. the pups should always be active, able to suckle strongly, and growing

    6. the pups should always be warm - cold puppies do not survive (air conditioning and keeping pups outside in cooler climates can be potential difficulties for young pups)

    7. any discharge that has an odor coming from the mother needs immediate care (this may be an indication of infection)

    8. within 24–48 hours after delivery of the pups, some veterinarians recommend an exam for the mother and pups -some veterinarians give the mother dog an injection of oxytocin to help the uterus shrink down and rid itself of any fluid or leftover afterbirths from the pups - a sooner appointment may be necessary if the mother or pups are showing any other signs than the normal signs listed here

CALCIUM CAUTION

Mother dogs' milk has calcium for the pups. While nursing, a mother's calcium level may decrease in her body, leading to a serious lowering of her calcium levels. The signs this may be occurring are:

1. shaking
2. seizures
3. muscle weakness
4. muscle tremors
5. inability to wake the mother up

Any of these signs or any abnormal signs in a mother dog indicates a need for her to be seen immediately by a veterinarian.

Some recommend calcium supplements after the pups are a few days old, and to continue for weeks while she is making milk for the pups.

Puppies are amazing and fun. Enjoy them.

Medications may be necessary while a dog is pregnant and/or nursing her pups.

Some medications may be harmful to growing or nursing puppies. And, even though not recommended for pregnant or nursing moms, may be necessary to save a mother dog's life and may be used regardless of the effect on her puppies.

MEDICATIONS SAFE FOR USE IN PREGNANT DOGS

Some medications SAFE for use in pregnancy and nursing dogs:
- activated charcoal
- artificial tears
- fenbendazole (Panacur)—dewormer
- ivermectin (Heartgard) — for the prevention of heartworm disease
- bismuth subsalicylate (Kaopectate) for diarrhea
- lufenuron (Program)—flea prevention medication
- milbemycin (Interceptor/Sentinel) for the prevention of fleas and heartworm disease
- pancreatic enzymes—that may be necessary for disease of the pancreas
- selamectin (Revolution)—for the prevention of fleas and heartworm disease
- thyroid medication—levothyroxine—for the treatment of low-functioning thyroid glands in the dog

MEDICATION NOT SAFE FOR USE IN PREGNANT DOGS

Some medications NOT recommended for pregnant or nursing dogs:

- acepromazine
- amitraz – found in Mitaban dips and Preventic collars
- amitryptiline (Elavil) for separation anxiety
- aluminum hydroxide- simethicone (Maalox)
- magnesium hydroxide (Milk of Magnesia)
- aspirin

(Continued)
- buspirone hydrochloride (BuSpar)
- butorphenol tartrate (Torbututrol) -for pain
- carprophen (Rimadyl)
- dextromethorphan (in Robitussin cough syrup)
- diazepam (Valium)
- dimenhydrinate (Dramamine)
- diphenhydramine (Benadryl)
- enrofloxacin (Baytril) (antibiotic)

More Medication NOT recommended for pregnant or nursing dogs:

- epsiprantel (Cestex) -tapeworm medication
- famotidine (Pepcid)
- fluoxetine (Prozac)
- furosemide (Lasix)
- prednisone
- prednisone and antihistamine (Temeril P)
- flea products (such as Advantage)
- melarsomine (Immiticide -used to treat heartworm disease)
- metronidazole (Flagyl)—antibiotic
- omeprazole (Prilosec)
- phenobarbital
- phenytoin (Dilantin)
- potassium bromide
- desoxyphenobarbital) Primidone
- vitamin K
- poly sulfated glycosaminoglycan (Adequan)

(Continued)

- amoxicillin/trihydrate/clavulanate (Clavamox) antibiotic
- ranitidine (Zantac)
- deprenyl (Selegiline) -used for older pets' aging brains
- sulpha antibiotics
- tetracycline/doxycycline—antibiotics
- potassium methylxanthine (in Theophylline and Aminophylline)

Also NOT recommended for pregnant and nursing mothers are the poisonous plants, household products, and medications listed in chapter 10.

Always consult a veterinarian for recommendation of medication use in pregnant or nursing dogs.

Chapter 7

DENTAL CARE

DID YOU KNOW...?

- dental disease is the most common condition in dogs.
- all pets are at risk for dental disease
- over 75% of dogs have dental disease by 3 years of age, and this incidence increases with age
- small breeds suffer more from dental disease than larger breeds
- the majority of owners do not provide essential dental care for pets
- we want you to be of the small percentage of pet owners who do provide dental care for their pets

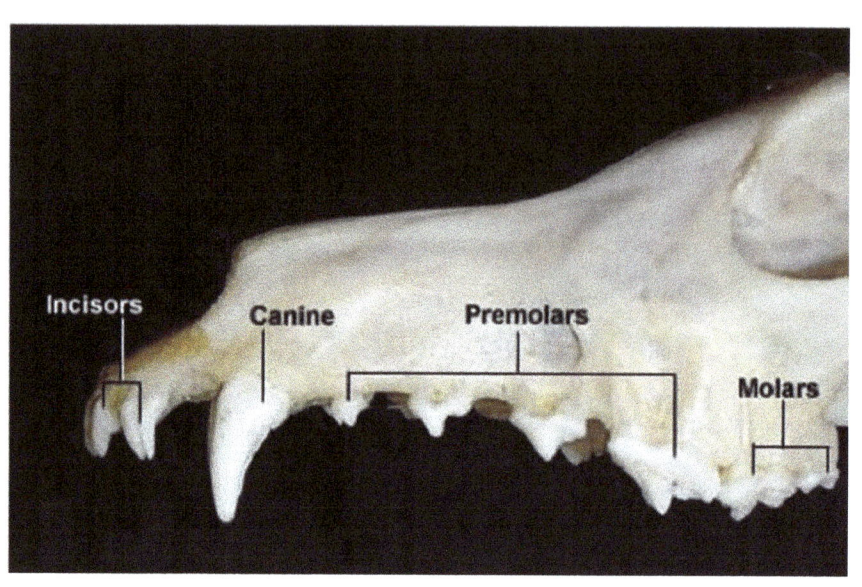

TOOTH ERUPTION

	DECIDUOUS	PERMANENT
Incisors	4–6 weeks	3–5 months
Canine	5–6 weeks	4–6 months
Premolars	6 weeks	4–5 months
Molars		5–7 months

Our pets need our help...

The key to dental health is to prevent the buildup of tartar on the teeth.

This chapter explores ways to save dental dollars and keep teeth healthier. Preventative care saves costly cleanings and possible extractions.

Aim to keep pets in the "no tartar" zone.

STAGES OF TARTAR BUILDUP

Dogs present daily with the following stages of dental needs:

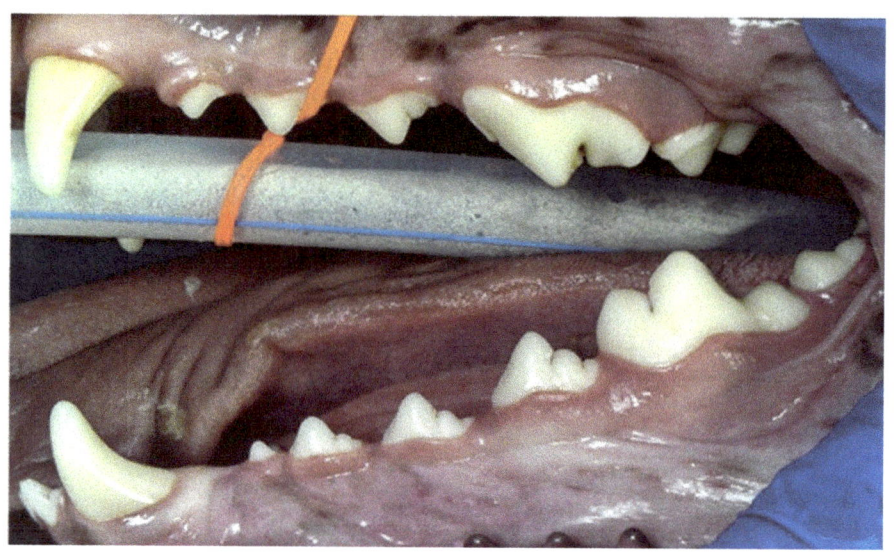

- no tartar

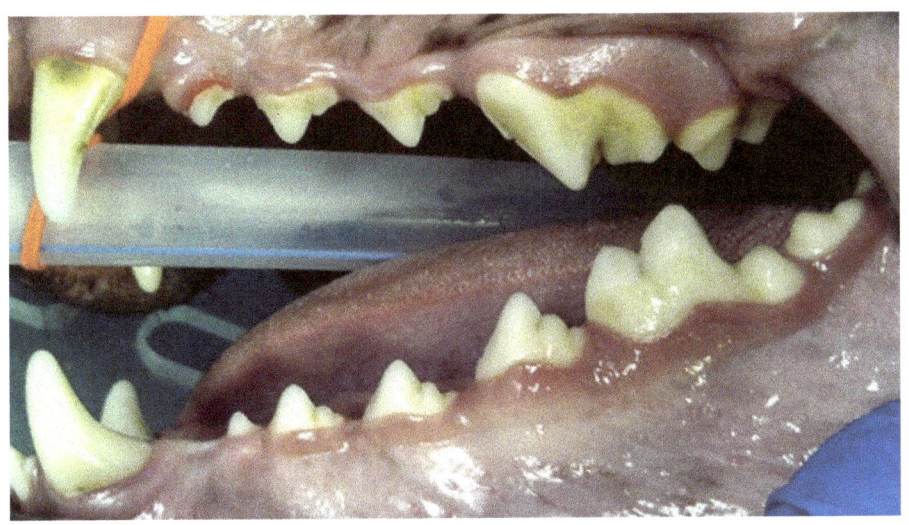

- mild tartar—this stage begins with plaque that accumulates and becomes rough and hardened with calcium to form tartar or calculus

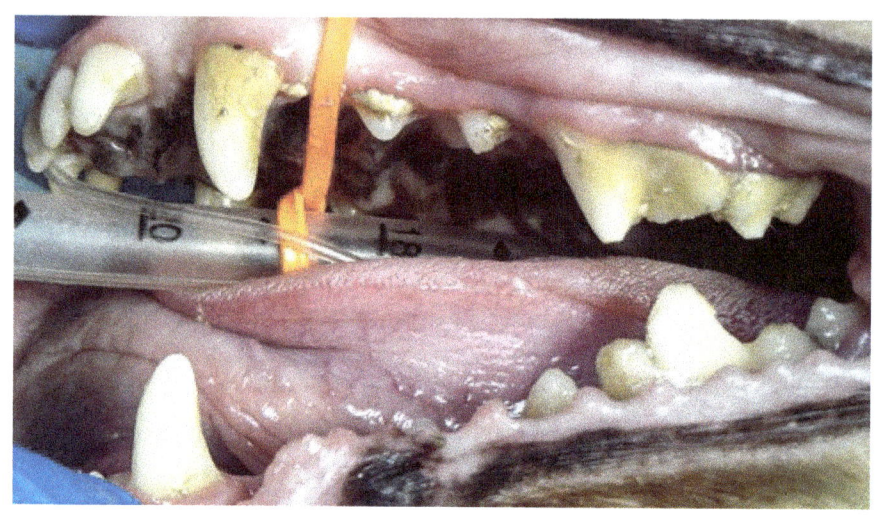

- more tartar—leading to gingivitis—which is an inflammation (irritation) of the gums that worsens over time

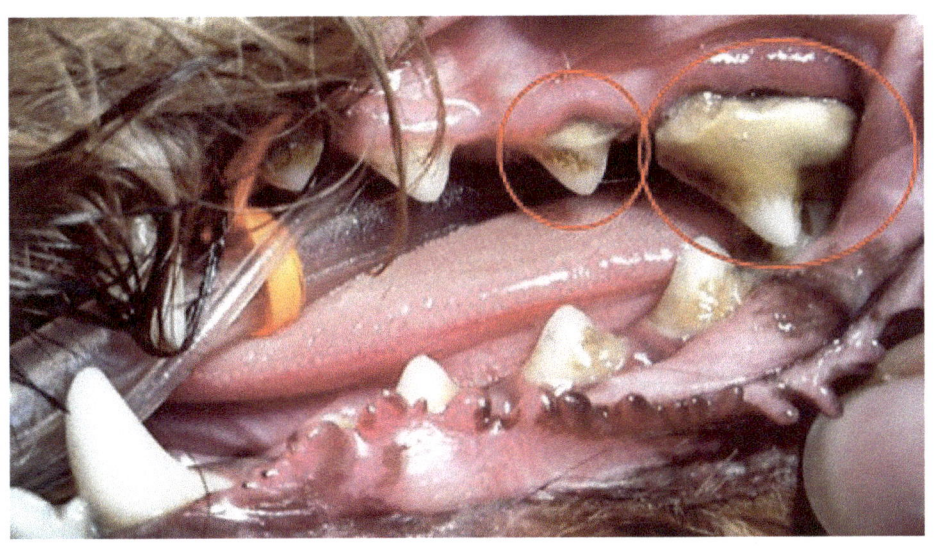

- much more tartar—as the accumulation of tartar progresses, the soft tissue and bone surrounding the affected tooth are destroyed and the tooth becomes loose—this is painful and leads to the loss of the tooth; however, this is preventable

SIGNS AND SYMPTOMS PETS NEED DENTAL CARE

Despite the best care given out pets, tartar may still accumulate. If and when dental tartar accumulates, cleaning and polishing under anesthesia is necessary with the possibility of extractions.

Signs a dog may need teeth cleaning are:
- bad breath
- change in eating habits—sometimes refusing to eat
- weight loss
- pain
- pawing at their face
- drooling
- loose and/or broken teeth
- exposed tooth roots
- red, swollen, bleeding, or painful gums
- sometimes facial swelling—especially under the pet's eyes
- obvious tartar

Teeth that are loose, decayed, and painful are removed. It is not recommended to allow these decayed teeth to remain in the mouths of the pets.

REASONS FOR DENTAL CARE

REASONS TO DO DENTAL CARE ARE:

- avoid costly cleanings
- dogs with healthy teeth live longer
- prevent pain to the dog's mouth which may result in pet's not eating and weight loss
- reduce chances of gum and bone infection from germs in the mouth
- prevent bad breath
- as in humans, poor dental health can contribute to disorders of the dog's heart, kidneys, liver, or other body areas

PREVENTATIVE CARE

Several tips to prevent the buildup of tartar on pets' teeth are:

- dental chews daily help massage the gums and prevent tartar build-up
- rinses—including antibacterial rinses added to drinking water
- toothpaste—only use toothpaste designed for dogs because human toothpaste is not recommended for dogs
- brushing 2–5 times weekly
- feeding dry dog food (hard kibble) if able
- giving toys designed for dental health
- dental diets help some pets
- dental examination every 6 months
- professional cleaning when needed
- having decayed or loose teeth removed

BRUSHING YOUR PET'S TEETH

You can train your dog to allow you to brush their teeth.

Tips for brushing are:

- begin to train a dog when they are young
- talk soothingly to your dog so they view brushing as a reward
- use a small pet brush or wrap a piece of gauze around a finger—use circular motions on the teeth, always stroking in a downward motion

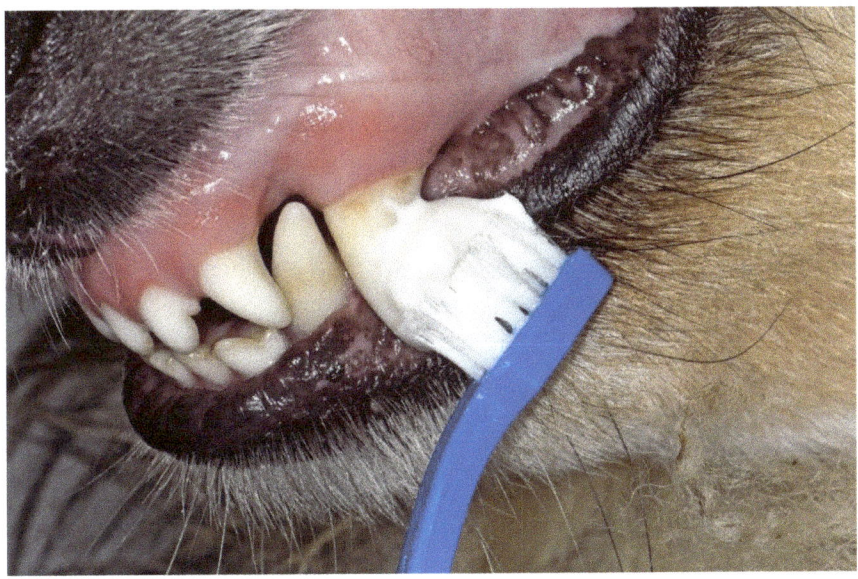

SOME INCLUDED DEFINITIONS

- Periodontal disease is a painful bacterial infection of the tissue around the tooth between the tooth and the gum, which can result in tooth loss and spread infection to the rest of the body. Signs are loose teeth, bad breath, tooth pain, sneezing and nasal discharge. Periodontal disease has progressive stages that are reversible and preventable.
- Gingivitis is an inflammation of the gums caused mainly by accumulation of plaque, tartar and disease-producing bacteria above and below the gum line. Signs include bleeding, red, swollen gums and bad breath. It is reversible and preventable with regular teeth cleanings.
- Halitosis—or bad breath—can be the first sign of a mouth problem and is caused by bacteria growing from food particles caught between the teeth or by gum infection. Regular tooth-brushings are a great solution.
- Swollen gums develop when tartar builds up and food gets stuck between the teeth. Regularly brushing your dog's teeth at home and getting annual cleanings at the vet can prevent tartar and gingivitis.
- Proliferating gum disease occurs when the gum grows over the teeth and must be treated to avoid gum infection. An inherited condition common to boxers and bull terriers, it can be treated with antibiotics.
- Mouth tumors appear as lumps in the gums. Some are malignant (harmful to the pet because they spred to other areas of the body) and are recommended to be surgically removed.
- Salivary cysts look like large, fluid-filled blisters under the tongue, but can also develop near the corners of the jaw. They require drainage, and the damaged saliva gland must be removed.

Chapter 8

NUTRITION

Proper nutrition can:
- help pets live longer
- help prevent dental disease and overweight pets
- help prevent arthritis and the pain associated with arthritis

GOAL: provide proper nutrition for dogs for all stages of pet development

STAGES OF DEVELOPMENT

OBJECTIVES OF PROPER NUTRITION FOR THE STAGES OF DEVELOPMENT:

To provide nutrition for body development of young growing puppies
- puppy diets are recommended for the first year of life

Provide energy for daily activities in young, active dogs
- adult diets are available
- as well, active formulas have been created for the active dogs

Provide nourishment for health and recovery as pets age:
- senior diets
- heart diets
- kidney diets
- food allergy diets
- bladder stone diets
- intestinal upset diets
- low-fat diets
- diabetic diets

Not only do we need to consider the age of our pets, but also their size. Extra small to giant breed dogs—each has special nutritional needs.

TYPES OF DIETS

IN ADDITION TO THE DIETS INCLUDED…

Owners may also choose:

- grain-free diets
- natural diets
- organic diets
- alternative protein diets—salmon, venison, and others
- about 1,000 more

and last, but not least…

WEIGHT MANAGEMENT DIETS

Diets provide nutrition for all stages of a pet's life. Veterinarians can help with choices available.

The focus of this chapter is different diets that help with weight management concerns.

Weight issues are often a sensitive subject for owners; however, weight is an important concern for our pets because:

       1. our pets' weights determine their overall health.
       2. weight can predict their life expectancy
       3. …and quality of life.

GOALS FOR WEIGHT MANAGEMENT

It is proven that overweight dogs are more prone to

       1. heart disease
       2. diabetes
       3. bone disease including arthritis
       4. and many other disorders

Diet, along with exercise and healthy snacks promotes great health and long life for dogs!

The GOAL in weight management is—
Not too thin, Not too fat, Just right.

Weight management diets are available as:

- low calorie foods
- healthy weight formulas
- reducing diets
- satiety diets
- and others

BODY CONDITIONING SCORES (BCS)

BCS is a scale used to evaluate body condition in dogs. Scoring is done by using numbers from 1 to 5.

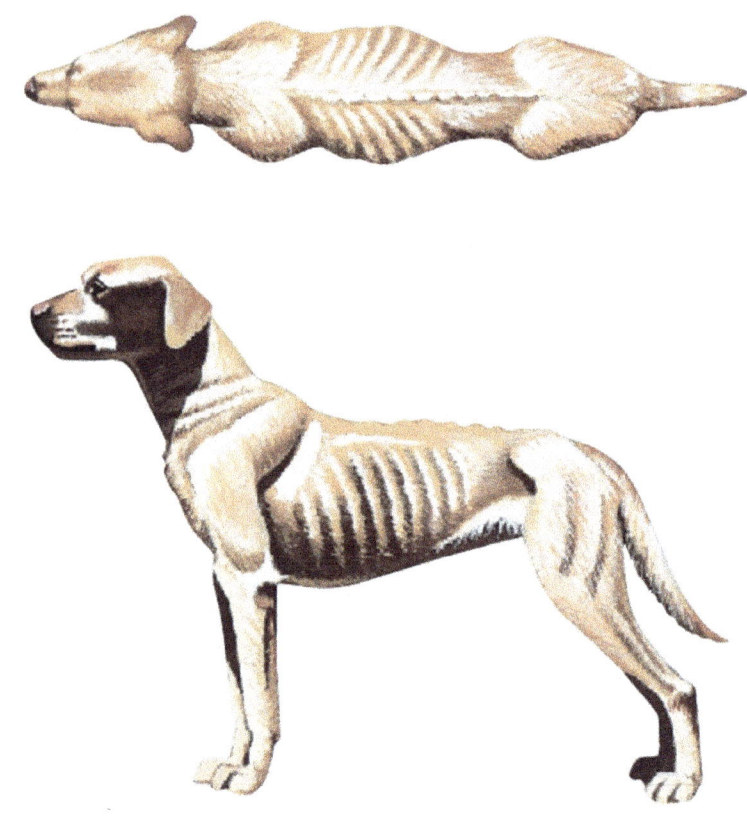

1 – very underweight

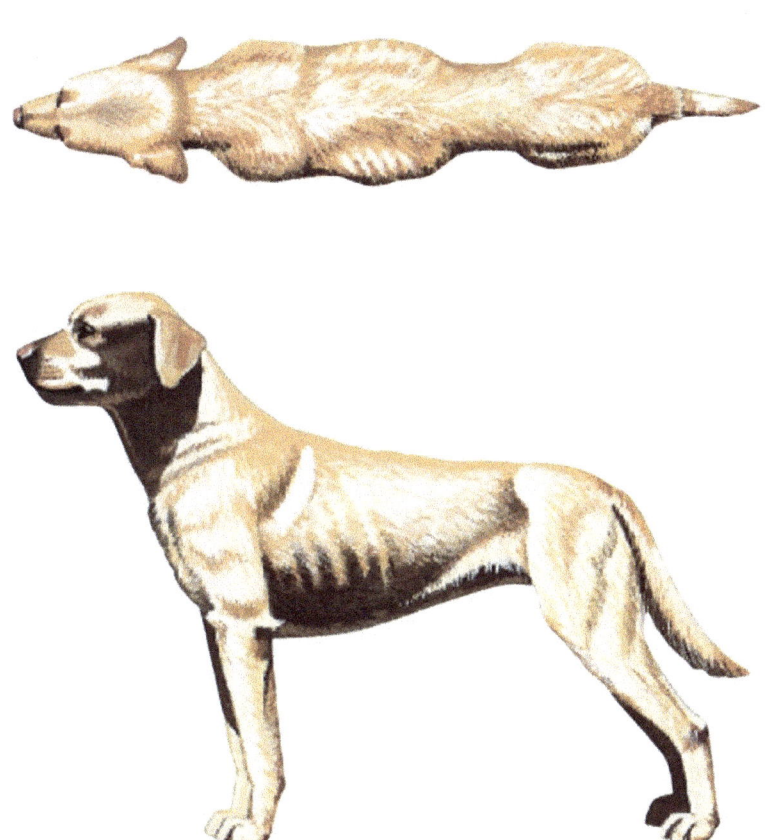

2 – slightly underweight

3 – perfect

4 – slightly overweight

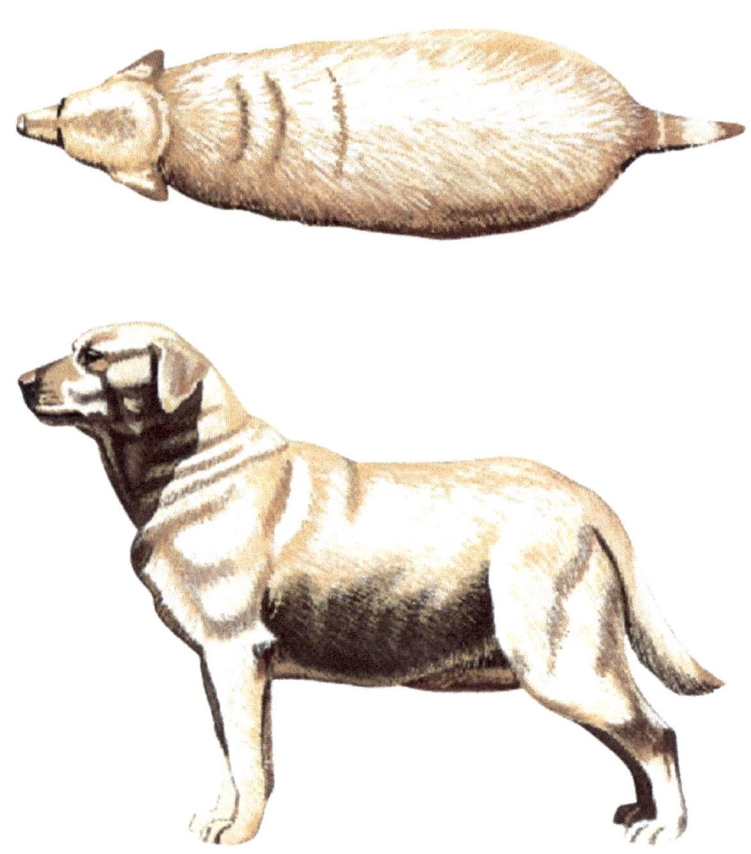

5 – very overweight

BENEFITS OF LOWER CALORIE FOODS

The BENEFITS of lower calorie pet foods are…

- less calories
- can feed a volume large enough for pet to feel full
- proper balanced nutrition

When pets are fed less of their current foods, the calories are reduced; however, so is the nutrition in the food as well.

TREATS

- are a great reward for our pets
- are a way for owners to bond with their pets
- help owners show a pet how much they are loved
- dogs love them and
- owners love giving their dogs treats.
- but treats can add additional and sometimes unwanted calories to a pet's diet

HEALTHY SNACKS

Healthy snacks that are lower calorie treats include baby carrots, green beans, broccoli and specially formulated low-calorie snacks made for dogs

Fruits such as bananas, watermelon, pieces of apple without the seeds, air-popped popcorn and rice cakes are also lower calorie alternatives to high-calorie snacks.

HOMEMADE TREATS

Making homemade treats has the following benefits:

1. owners can control the ingredients of the treats and can modify treats for dietary restrictions of pets
2. the treats can be made nutritious
3. treats can be tailored to taste preferences
4. it is possible to avoid unhealthy additives when no preservatives are used to make the treats
5. the treats are lower in calories

Treats can be made from canned specialty diets where the soft food is pressed onto a cookie sheet, cut into shapes, baked until firm, removed from the oven and stored for treat giving.

Additional homemade treats are included on the following pages. All recipes can be doubled or tripled for additional treats per batch of treat making.

Basic dog biscuits

- 1 1/4 cups whole wheat flour (regular or oats if the pet is sensitive to wheat)
- 1/2 tsp salt (or less)
- 1 egg
- 1/2 tsp of beef or chicken bouillon granules (or beef or chicken broth/stock)
- 1/4 cup hot water

Directions:
- preheat oven to 350 degrees
- dissolve bouillon in hot water
- add remaining ingredients
- knead dough until 1/2 inch thick
- cut into slices or bone shapes (with a bone cookie cutter)
- cook 30 minutes
- you may double or triple the recipe for larger numbers of treats

Healthy pumpkin balls

This snack is healthy and filled with fiber, vitamin A, beta-carotene, iron, and potassium.
- 1/4 cup of canned pumpkin
- 2 T molasses
- 2 T water
- 1 T vegetable oil
- 1 cups whole wheat flour
- 1/8 tsp baking soda
- 1/8 tsp baking powder
- 1/2 tsp cinnamon (optional)

Directions:
- preheat to 350 degrees
- mix pumpkin, molasses, water, and vegetable oil together in a bowl
- add the flour, baking powder, baking soda, and cinnamon to the mix and stir until the dough softens
- scoop out small spoonfuls of dough and roll into balls with your hands (wet hands work best)
- set the balls onto a lightly greased cookie sheet and flatten out the sheet.
- bake approx. 25 minutes until dough is hardened

This recipe may be doubled or tripled for larger numbers of treats.

Apple crunch pupcakes

- 1 1/2 cups water
- 1/8 cup unsweetened applesauce
- 1 T honey
- 1/8 tsp of vanilla extract
- 1 medium egg
- 2 cups of whole wheat flour
- 1/2 cup of dried apple chips (unsweetened)
- 1/2 tsp baking soda

Directions:
- preheat oven to 350 degrees
- mix water, honey, applesauce, egg, and vanilla together in a bowl
- add remaining ingredients and mix until well blended
- pour into lightly greased muffin pans
- bake 1 1/4 hours

This recipe may be doubled or tripled to make increased numbers of treats.

To keep treats fresher, longer, place treats in airtight containers and freeze.

Treats can last up to 6 months in the freezer.

Try ingredients out before making a big batch.

Thaw 10–15–20 minutes prior to feeding.

Healthy snack
- 1/2 medium ripe banana
- 1/2 cup shredded carrots (shredding yourself with allow the skins to remain on, if purchase shredded carrots- will need to make even smaller)
- 1/8 cup applesauce, unsweetened
- 1/8 cup water (an additional 1/8 cup may be needed)
- 3/4 cups whole wheat flour
- 1 cup rolled oats

(additional flour for rolling)

Directions:
- preheat oven to 350 degrees
- mash the ripe banana in a small bowl
- grate the carrots, and mix with the banana
- pour in the applesauce and water
- in a medium bowl, whisk together the flour and oats
- make a well in the center of the dry ingredients and pour in the carrot mixture
- stir until thoroughly combined
- knead the dough in the bowl with your hands
- fold out onto a floured surface and continue to knead until the dough has formed
- roll out to 1/2- inch thickness
- cut into 3-inch pieces (or use a carrot-shaped cookie cutter)
- lightly spray a baking sheet with non-stick spray
- place the cut-outs on the baking sheet and bake for 25 minutes
- let them cool on a wire rack

Will keep in refrigerator for 3 weeks,
or in the freezer for up to 6 months.

Owners may double or triple this recipe for more treats.

For crunchy snack—leave in oven overnight after done cooking and oven turned off.

Pumpkin and peanut butter treats
- 1/4 14 oz can pumpkin
- 1 1/2 T peanut butter (do not use peanut butter sweetened with xylitol)
- 2 egg whites or 1 whole egg (less calories with the egg whites)
- 1/4 tsp of salt
- 1/4 tsp of cinnamon
- 1/4 to 1/2 cup water
- 1 1/2 cups whole wheat flour

Directions:
- preheat oven to 350 degrees
- add 1/4 of the 14 oz can of pumpkin to 2 egg whites, 1/4 cup water, 1 1/2 t peanut butter, 1/4 tsp salt, and 1/4 tsp cinnamon
- turn on the mixer and combine until well mixed
- slowly add 1 1/2 cups of flour with the mixer on level 2 speed
- add a little more water to get all the flour incorporated (usually another 1/4 cup); this is very dry dough
- place the dough on a cutting surface, cut into 4 equal pieces.
- roll into logs of 1-inch diameter
- cut into ½-inch pieces (about 60 bones)
- prep 2 large cookie sheets with parchment paper and distribute the biscuits evenly
- bake for 30 minutes for semi-hard

Chapter 9

ARTHRITIS

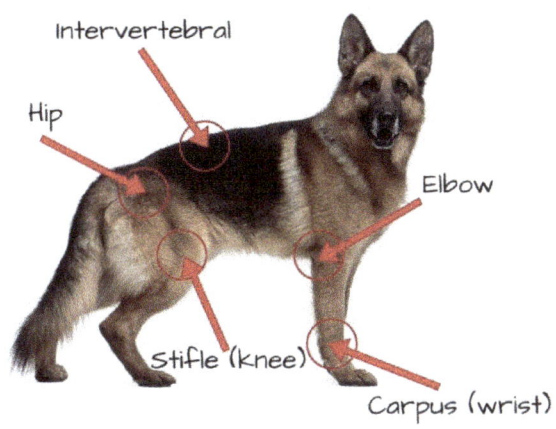

Arthritis is an irritation in a joint that is not curable and will continually worsen.

Arthritis is common—1 out of 5 dogs has arthritis.

Arthritis causes changes in the bone and cartilage at the ends of bones that are included in joints (where two bones come together).

Arthritis leads to pain and difficulty rising or moving—which decreases the quality of the pet's life.

Every age dogs can have arthritis; however, mostly older and overweight pets develop arthritis.

Hips are not the only joint in a dog's body that can develop arthritis—any joint may be affected, including the elbow, the knee (stifle), the spine, or any joint.

TYPES OF ARTHRITIS

The different types of arthritis include:

1. degenerative (the most common type—AKA osteoarthritis)
2. rheumatoid (a condition where the body attacks its own tissue)
3. and infectious arthritis (caused by infectious agents such as bacteria)

SIGNS OF ARTHRITIS

Signs of arthritis include:

- decrease in his/her activity and playfulness
- getting up slowly
- seemingly quiet and sad
- crying or whimpering as he/she walks—especially when just rising from a lying position
- yelping in pain if the affected joint/s is/are manipulated
- reluctance to climb stairs
- swelling in affected joints
- potential for an elevated temperature
- walking stiffly or limping on one or more legs
- lowering of the back legs if the hips are affected
- little muscle mass in the rear areas if the hips and lower spine are affected
- increased muscle mass to the front legs when the pet uses this area for support to decrease pressure to painful rear or back joints

GOALS FOR PET OWNERS

GOALS for pet owners with arthritic dogs are:

- having knowledge of arthritis
- being aware of available treatments
- knowing treatment recommendations change as pets age
- knowing the benefits and risks of all treatments
- knowing the proper administration of all treatments
- having a good relationship with your veterinarian

TREATMENT FOR ARTHRITIS

Treatments for arthritis include, but are not limited to:

Joint supplements may be effective in prevention of arthritis and/or early stages of arthritis and include:

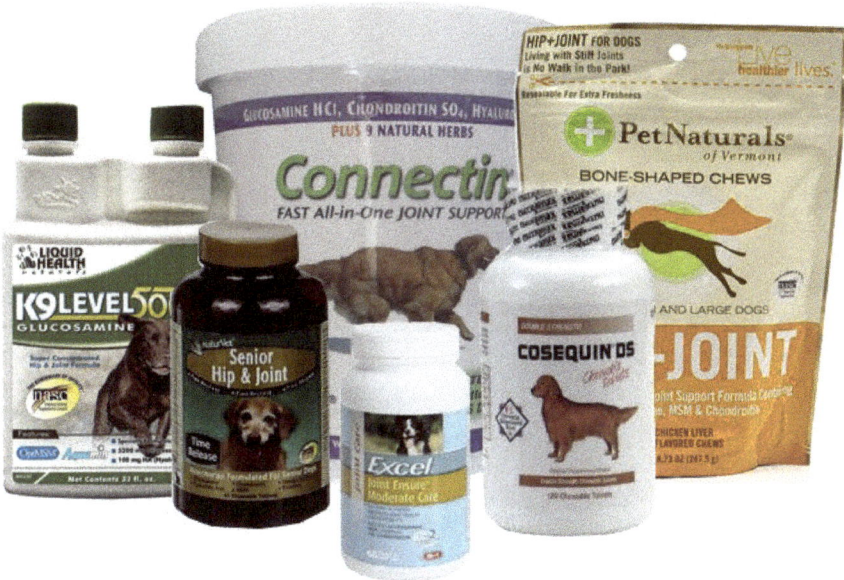

- nutritional support- there are specially formulated diets for joint health
- nutraceuticals- including glucosamine and chondroitin – these are chemicals found in the cartilage of healthy joints- these supplements help protect joints
- polysulfated glycosaminoglycan- (Adequan)- is a medication given by injection- frequently at first, then less often- this medication helps protect the cartilage found at the ends of the bones within joints

When arthritis becomes more advanced, medications may be recommended and include:

- NSAIDS- which are non- steroidal anti inflammatory drugs- are medications that, as the name states, are not cortisone or prednisone-type medications used for pain relief in joints- examples of these include carprophen or metacam – these medications can sometimes make a pet play like a puppy again
- Tramadol – is another medication sometimes recommended for arthritic discomfort

Some common non-medication therapies include:

- heat application
- cold application
- manipulation of the muscles and joints- physical therapy- by moving the joints in all motions natural to the joint, exercising the pet's limbs and joints while massaging them
- water therapy is also a great way to exercise a dog without stress to the joints- always walk or swim in water with a life vest on and monitor (supervise) the pet at all times

Other therapies include… do not go to sleep yet, this is good stuff...

- TENS- a unit applied to provide electrical stimulation
- lasers- which apply heat and vibration for comfort
- ultrasound
- shock waves
- magnets
- therapeutic exercise
- acupuncture
- herbs
- antibiotics if infection is present
- omega 3's
- lifestyle changes

In advanced arthritis veterinarians may recommend:

- steroids such as prednisone
- immune suppressive medication may be indicated in rheumatoid arthritis
- or surgery may be recommended – such as hip removals or replacements, spine surgeries, and others

On the horizon is very advanced research including:

- adipose – derived stem cell therapy
- and cartilage transplants

Arthritis is common and can be costly. It may be preventable or delayed with early care as noted.

Also, the most effective way an owner can prevent arthritis is by managing their pet's weight.

Chapter 10
POISONS

Many common household foods, plants, and products are poisonous to dogs.

Even therapeutic medication and flea products can be harmful if a pet is sensitive or allergic to the medication or product, or if they are administered incorrectly.

SIGNS OF POISONING

If a pet is poisoned, some signs include:

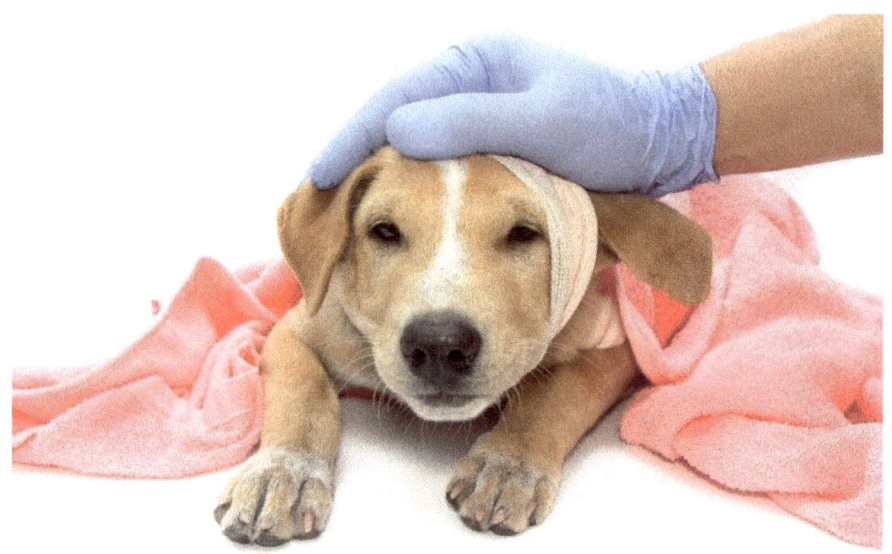

- vomiting
- diarrhea
- abnormalities in urine—in the color, odor, frequency, or amount
- salivation
- staggering
- bleeding
- coma—unable to arouse a pet
- weakness
- seizures
- tremors
- change in mental status—appearing disoriented, confused
- difficulty breathing
- loss of pet

FOODS TO AVOID

- raw bread dough (yeast dough)
- almonds
- apple seeds
- plums
- pits of apricots, cherries, and peaches
- gum or other foods such as peanut butter with xylitol (an artificial sweetener)
- chocolate
- drinking alcohol—including HOPS

MORE FOODS TO AVOID:

- grapes and raisins
- macadamia nuts
- walnuts
- moldy foods
- onions, onion powder, and chives
- garlic
- scallions
- persimmons
- some mushrooms—the types toxic to humans
- coffee—the grounds, beans, and chocolate-covered beans

HOUSEHOLD ITEMS TO AVOID

- antifreeze
- acetaminophen -(Tylenol)
- prescription medications
- human vitamins
- isopropyl alcohol
- de-icing salts
- compost piles
- drain cleaners
- bleach
- boric acid
- deodorants
- ant traps
- insect control products
- shoe polish
- sleeping pills
- turpentine

MORE HOUSEHOLD ITEMS TO AVOID:

- rat poison
- vitamins
- weed killers
- windshield wiper fluid
- pennies—post 1982 (due to zinc content)
- furniture polish
- hair color
- matches
- liquid potpourri
- snail bait—even when placed under plants outdoors
- batteries
- flea products used WRONGLY
- detergents
- fertilizers
- insecticides
- household cleaners
- kerosene
- all petroleum products—oil, gasoline
- moth balls

PLANTS AND SHRUBS TO AVOID

- poinsettias
- azaleas
- rhododendrons
- oleander
- english ivy
- amaryllis (Hippeastrum species and hybrids)
- chrysanthemum
- crown of thorns (euphorbia milii)
- cyclamen (kalanchoe)
- gardenia (gardenia augusta, g. jasminoides)
- geranium (pelargonium species)
- hyacinth (hyacinthus species and hybrids)
- primrose (primula vulgaris)
- baby's breath (gypsophila paniculata)
- daffodil (narcissus species)
- dahlia
- gladiola (some gladiolus varieties)
- holly (Ilex species)
- iris species
- mistletoe (many genera)
- naked lady (amaryllis belladonna)
- peony (paeonia species)

MORE PLANTS AND SHRUBS TO AVOID:

- tulip (tulipa species)
- begonia
- jade plant
- asparagus fern
- corn plant
- satin pothos (silk pothos)
- carnations
- elephant ear
- tomato and potato leafs and stems
- morning glories
- dumb cane (dieffenbachia amoena)
- Norfolk Island pine (araucaria heterophylla)
- philodendron (most)
- rubber plant (ficus elastica)
- hostas
- rhubarb
- sago palm (cycas revoluta)
- shamrock (oxalis)
- milk weed
- wild cherry
- narcissus bulbs
- aloe vera

WHAT TO DO IF A PET IS POISONED

Many emergency clinics are available for assistance if your pet requires care. Always seek help immediately. The quicker treatment is sought, the better chance a pet can survive a poisonous exposure.

Always have emergency phone numbers available—Veterinary Emergency Clinics and Poison Hotlines.

One Pet Poison Helpline is 800-213-6680.

Chapter 11

TRAINING

Who doesn't love a well-trained dog?

Many talented owners train their dogs to:

- sit
- stay
- come
- bring the paper
- walk on a leash or harness

Some extra talented owners teach their dogs to:

- retrieve drinks from the refrigerator
- walk the children
- babysit the children
- make 911 calls
- operate the computer
- fall to the ground when pretending to shoot them (always fun at parties)

Other talented trainers teach dogs to:

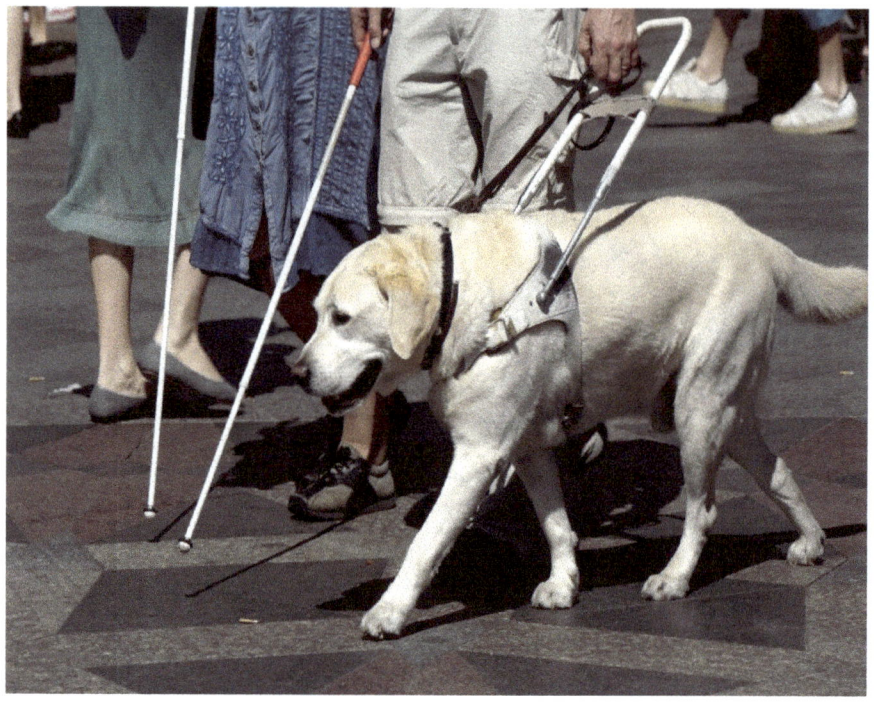

- rescue people in need—lost children, search and rescue
- become guide dogs for the visually impaired
- service dogs for multiple medical needs of owners

HOW TO SOCIALIZE YOUR PETS

WAYS TO SOCIALIZE AND TRAIN PETS ARE:

- be informed—get books from the library or contact a trainer
- enroll in puppy training classes
- be consistent
- be kind
- socialize pet with people and other pets as much as possible before 6 months of age
- make experiences positive—traveling to fun places and not only to the veterinarian, giving treats when traveling or mixing with others
- avoid negative behaviors as much as possible
- seek assistance early when a problem is identified
- crate-train young pets

MORE WAYS TO SOCIALIZE AND TRAIN PETS:

- use positive reinforcement for good behavior
- avoid biting play with human hands—always offer a toy a pet may chew on when they try to mouth or chew on your hand
- enjoy much play time with your pet
- give your pet toys that are theirs to play with
- exercise them frequently
- train them to leash/harness walk at an early age
- engage them in sports or activities appropriate for their breed—such as herding for herding dogs, swimming for retrievers, and other activities

Medications are available if needed.

Training bonds you to your dog.

AS MUCH FUN AS TRAINING IS.....

Behavioral issues may be the most frequent reasons a pet is surrendered to a shelter.

It is sad when objectionable behavior that can be avoided leads to separation of pet and owner.

Dogs are not born bad.

Dogs can succumb to boredom or separation anxiety.

FREQUENTLY ENCOUNTERED BEHAVIORAL ISSUES

- aggression towards other pets and/or humans
- inappropriate urination
- separation anxiety that can lead to property destruction
- chewing inappropriate items—applies to puppies and older pets as well
- food aggression
- barking
- jumping up
- digging in the yard
- stealing food off counters
- jumping on furniture
- escaping—bolting out doors
- running the neighborhood
- pulling on leashes
- biting
- eating feces (stool, poop)
- eating objects such as leashes, toys and clothing that could result in a need for surgery to remove

Our goal is to help owners prevent the loss of pets for behavior issues.

Chapter 12

DIAGNOSTIC TESTING

A CLOSER LOOK

The first tool a veterinarian has to decide what disorders a dog may be experiencing is the physical exam.

The exam is important; however, it does not provide all the necessary information to make decisions about disorders and care recommendations, and a closer look is necessary.

Tests are available which help veterinarians make accurate decisions about disorders dogs experience—and therefore more accurate treatment recommendations.

Understanding the testing often recommended may be helpful to owners in making decisions regarding their pets' care.

COMMON TESTS RECOMMENDED

Some common tests recommended are:

1. blood tests for heartworm disease
2. fecal samples (AKA poop samples)
3. blood tests to count cells
4. blood tests for screening body organs
5. measuring electrolytes
6. blood tests for irritation of the pancreas
7. thyroid testing
8. measuring bile acids
9. testing adrenal gland function
10. tests to measure a pet's ability to clot blood
11. diabetes mellitus testing
12. radiographs—x-rays
13. advanced testing—ultrasounds, MRIs, CT scans
14. skin testing
15. biopsies and fine needle aspiration
16. allergy testing
17. cultures
18. urine testing
19. ear testing
20. eye testing

HEARTWORM DISEASE

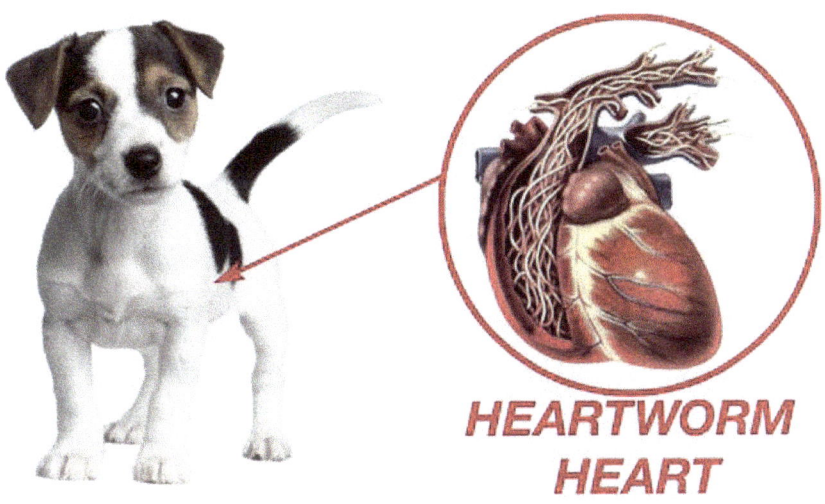

Heartworm is a serious disorder where "white spaghetti-like" worms live in the heart of infected dogs. These worms can cause heart and lung disease. They can also cause loss of a pet.

Heartworm infection begins with an infected dog.

We will call the infected dog **Dog A**. This dog has adult (mature) heartworms in their heart.

These adult worms make offspring—babies, called microfilaria—that float throughout the bloodstream.

DOG A

When a mosquito comes along and takes a blood meal from a dog with heartworm disease, it picks up the microfilaria—the "babies."

DOG A

When the mosquito then travels to another dog—whom we will call **Dog B**—that does not have heartworm to take its next blood meal, it deposits these microfilaria (immature larvae, or babies) into this new dog's skin.

DOG B

Over a few months, these immature worms grow and develop and then travel to the newly infected dog's heart.

Now **Dog B** also has heartworm disease.

SIGNS OF HEARTWORM DISEASE

Some signs of heartworm infection include:

….no signs of any disease to…

1. coughing
2. difficulty breathing
3. difficulty exercising or weakness
4. weight loss
5. unthrifty pet
6. and if not treated, the dog will be lost

Testing for heartworms is done by drawing a blood sample and completing a special test.

TREATING HEARTWORM DISEASE

IF POSITIVE FOR HEARTWORMS:

Veterinarians evaluate pets individually to make treatment recommendations.

In addition to medications to treat heartworms, testing is recommended to evaluate the overall health of a pet before making treatment recommendations.

Treatment in healthy dogs focuses on treating the adult worms in the heart and the microscopic offspring in the heart.

Treatment is costly and can be difficult and risky for pets.

PREVENTING HEARTWORM DISEASE

The GOAL in heartworm prevention is to eliminate immature larvae stages in the skin before they are able to mature into adult worms that travel to the heart.

This goal is accomplished by breaking the cycle of the heartworm infection with medication that kills any larvae that may be deposited in a pet's skin.

The medications available are:

1. spot ons
2. oral pills and chews
3. and a 6 month injection is available

Since heartworm microfilariae are microscopic and cannot be seen in a dog's skin, it is recommended that all dogs over 8 weeks old be on heartworm prevention all year and be tested regularly for heartworm disease.

Prevention saves cost and is safe for pets.

FECAL TESTS

Veterinarians examine feces (AKA stool, poop, and other homespun terms) to test for several common infections such as:

1. intestinal parasites—AKA "worms"
2. giardia
3. coccidia

COMMON INTESTINAL WORMS IN DOGS

COMMON NAME	SCIENTIFIC NAME
rounds	Toxocara spp.
hooks	Ancylostoma spp.
whips	Trichuris spp.
tapeworms (tapes)	Dipylidium and Tenia

Various medications are used to treat each type of "worm" a dog may be infected with.

Intestinal parasites require treatment because they cause:

- poor growth
- dull coat
- loss of weight
- lack of energy
- diarrhea
- vomiting
- lack of appetite
- pot belly appearance
- and loss of pets is possible when large numbers of worms are present

An additional and important reason to identify and treat worms is that they can be a health hazard to children and adults.

ROUNDWORMS

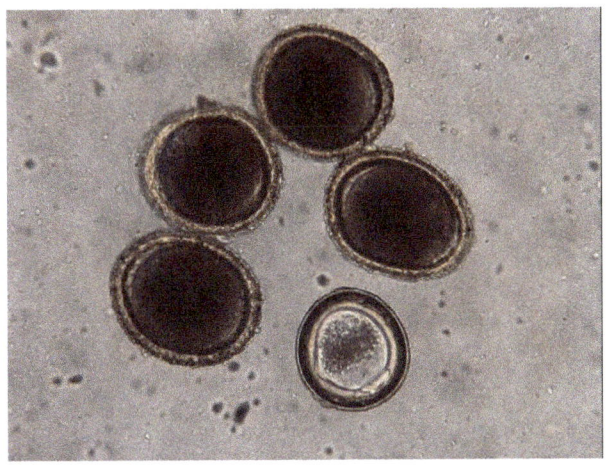

Roundworms ("Rounds") are the most commonly seen parasite in dogs—especially puppies. They are transmitted to puppies from their moms through the placenta before birth and the mother's milk after birth.

Rounds can be seen as white curly worms in stool or vomit that look like spaghetti.

HOOKWORMS

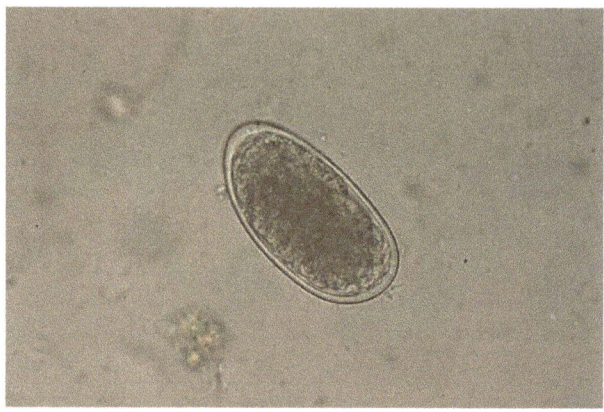

Hookworms are so small they can only be seen under a microscope.

They are serious because they damage the lining of the intestines when they attach there.

The main source of infection for dogs is usually soil contaminated with stool of infected pets; however, some hookworm infections are transmitted in mother's milk to nursing pups.

Additional symptoms seen in hookworm infection include:

1. severe illness
2. anemia
3. blood in the pet's stool
4. poor absorption of nutrition because of the damage to the lining of the intestinal tract—which can cause weight loss
5. this worm can be life-threatening if untreated.

WHIPWORMS

Whipworms ("Whips"), like hookworms, can only be seen under a microscope and are very serious worms in a dog.

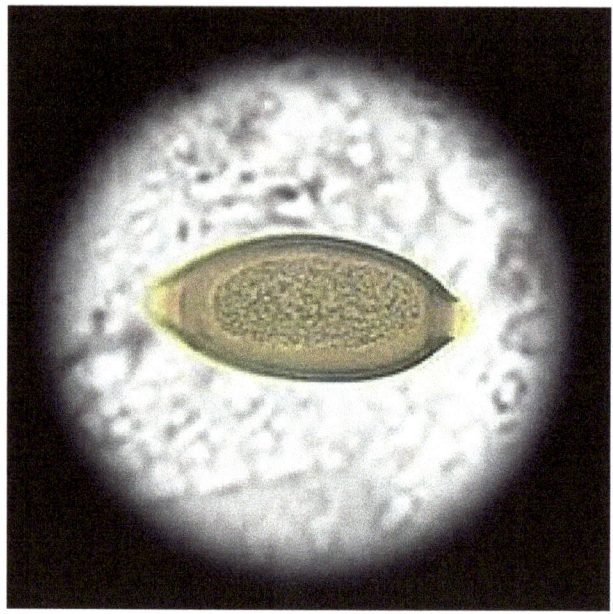

Since whipworms do not shed eggs in the stool consistently, it may require multiple stool examinations to detect these parasites.

Whips are serious because they:

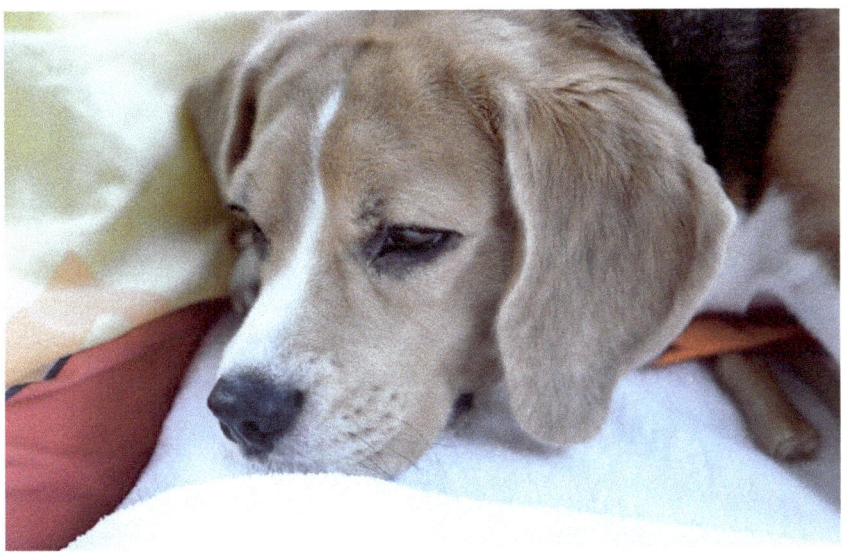

1. damage the lining of the intestinal tract
2. cause severe diarrhea with or without blood
3. cause dogs to become thin and unhealthy
4. cause a decreased appetite
5. and if untreated, these worms can be life-threatening

TAPEWORMS

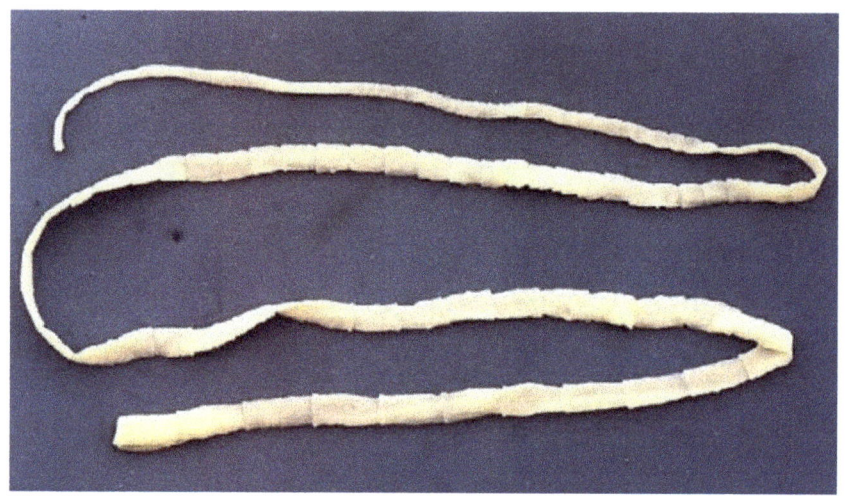

The 3 parts of a tapeworm are:

1. the head—which attaches to the intestinal lining
2. the neck
3. and the segments—which are passed and seen in the stool

Unlike other "worms," tapeworms are not passed directly from dog to dog—an "intermediate" or "in between" host is required for infection.

The segments are passed in the pet's stool, are identified as flat white worms or "rice" on a pet's stool or hair, and these segments contain tapeworm eggs.

These eggs are distributed in the environment and picked up by fleas and other possible hosts (such as rodents).

When a dog grooms itself and swallows fleas, the tapeworms develop into an adult worm and attach to the lining of the intestines—creating a new infection and cycle.

Treatment is available for tapes and is necessary because as long as the head of the tapeworm is attached to the lining of the intestinal tract, the dog is unable to digest and eliminate the worms themselves.

Tapeworms are not always detected on fecal examination, so many veterinarians treat when owners see these worms on their pets' stool.

Treatment is necessary because tapeworms can cause a pet to be ill or unthrifty.

Treatment for tapeworms is aimed at controlling flea infestations as well as treating the tapeworms.

Recommended treatment for fleas includes:

- treating all pets in the home all year
- cleaning all surfaces and bedding related to the pet in the home
- treating the environment if possible (the yard)

GIARDIA AND COCCIDIA

When testing feces, two other intestinal parasites may be a concern:

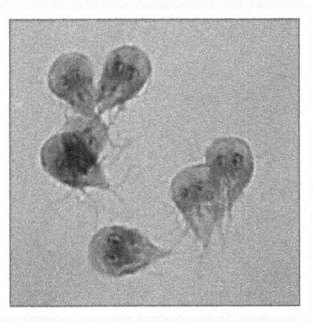

- **Giardia** is a small single cell organism that causes diarrhea in dogs and can be seen on a fecal examination or diagnosed with a special test.

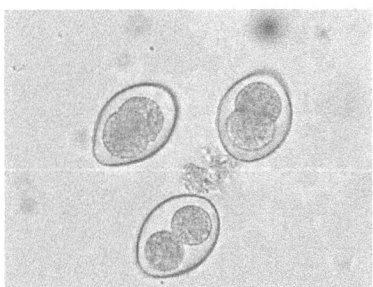

- **Coccidia** is a single-cell organism—a protozoa—that can only be seen under a microscope.

Medication is available to treat both giardia and coccidia. Treatment is essential to avoid serious complications that can result with each of these infections.

BLOODWORK

In addition to heartworm testing, veterinarians may recommend examining blood for the following:

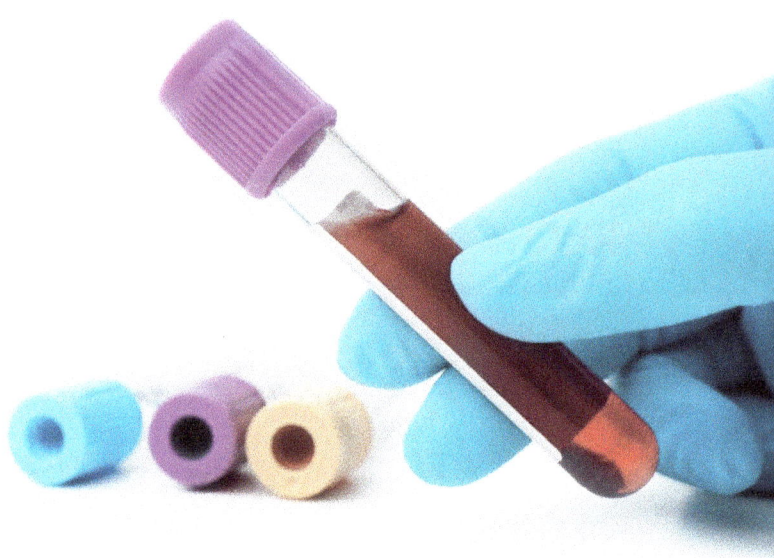

- complete Blood Counts—known as a CBC
- chemistry panels—known as SMAC, internal organ function, chem- 7,12, 15
- electrolytes—including sodium, chloride, and potassium
- pancreatic testing
- thyroid examination—most often a T4
- bile acids
- adrenal gland testing
- diabetic mellitus testing
- and others

Normal and Abnormal Blood Values

Normal and abnormal test results have value to veterinarians in the care of pets.

When evaluating blood values, there are standards called "normal" values. Health is when the values are normal, and disease may be identified when values are either too high or too low.

In addition, often testing may be:

- conclusive—give enough information to conclude what is wrong with the pet
- suggestive—a disorder may be apparent, but need further testing to be absolutely certain
- inconclusive—some tests could indicate more than one disorder, so other testing is necessary to be certain

Suggestive and inconclusive testing indicates a need for additional testing or referral to specialists for assistance with identifying disorders in dogs.

FACTS ABOUT BLOOD

When blood is placed in a spinner and spun, it separates into 3 parts:

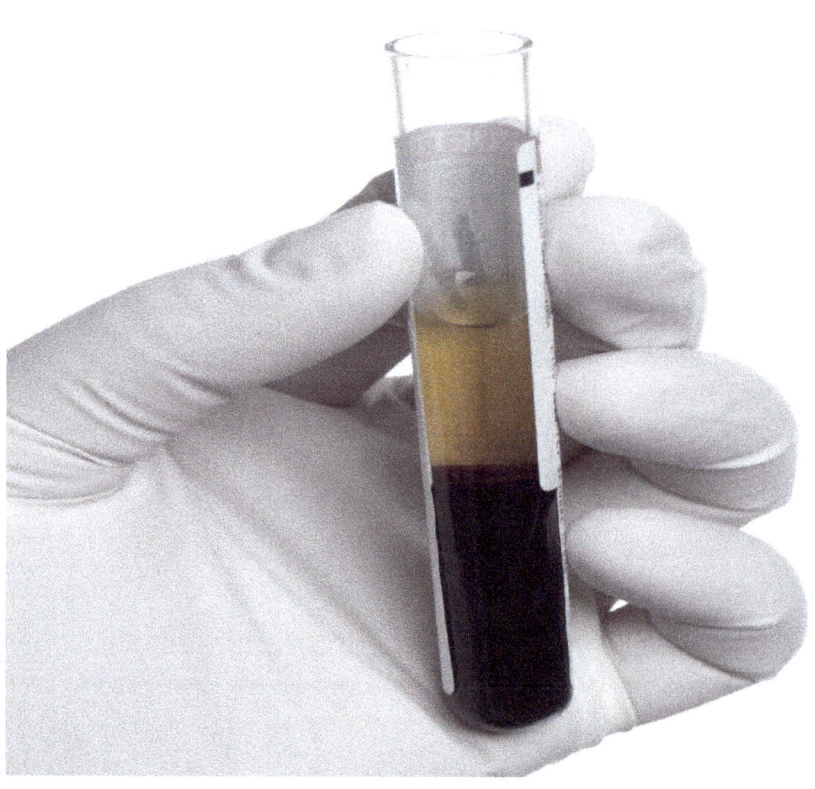

1. the liquid part that normally looks clear or slightly straw-colored
2. the red blood cells—which settle to the bottom
3. the white blood cells—a small layer of cells which are usually in the layer between the liquid part and the red blood cell

These parts of the blood are tested

COMPLETE BLOOD COUNTS

CBC – the complete blood count

The cells counted are:

1. the red cells—which carry oxygen n the blood
2. the platelets—which help with blood clotting
3. the white blood cells—there are 5 different types which help protect pets by fighting infection and other things (cancer)

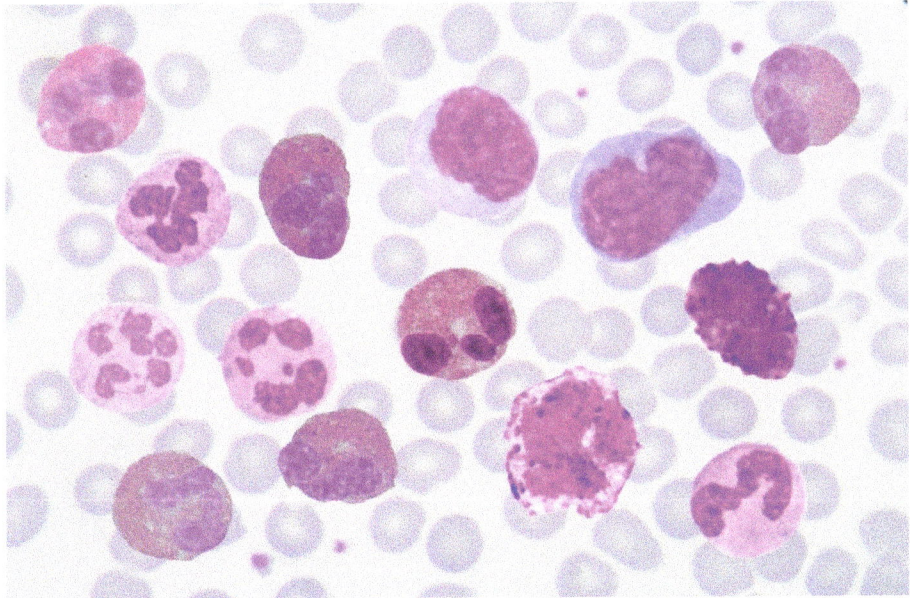

Veterinarians gain information when cell counts are:

- too high
- too low
- or just right (normal)

With this information, the veterinarian can create treatment plans for the care of pets.

CHEMISTRY

"Chemistry" tests are performed on the liquid part of blood and screen different items.

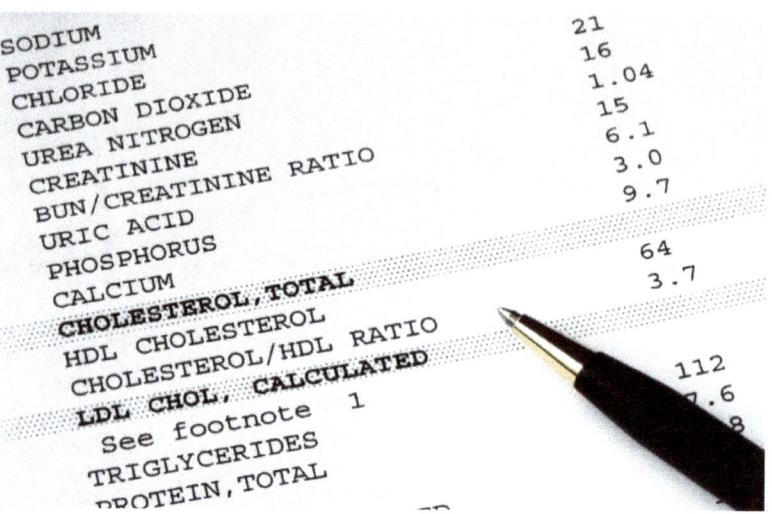

Some items relate to blood levels, reflecting organ health such as liver and kidney health; and some values relate to sugar in the blood, calcium, and even cholesterol. When these screening values are not within a normal range, illness is usually indicated—as well as the need for treatment and/or further testing or referral to specialists to decide what disorders may be present.

Several different chemistry "panels" are available—the number associated with the chemistry panel usually indicates how many items are being tested—for example:

Chem 6 – tests 6 basic items in the blood
Chem 12 – tests 12 items
Chem 25 – tests 25 items

And so on…

It is easy to see that the more items tested for, the more information is obtained.

Additional Tests on the Chemistry Panel

As with the CBC, there are "normal" standards established for the chemistry items tested for. Values that are "too high" or "too low" may indicate a need for treatment.

Some "chemistry" items tested are:

- Glucose – AKA blood sugar
- Creatinine – screens for kidney health
- BUN – the "blood urea nitrogen" – screens for kidney health
- ALT (alanine aminotransferase) – screens for liver health
- AST (aspartate aminotransferase) – screens for liver health
- GGT (gamma glutamyltransferase) – screens for liver health
- Albumin – a protein found in the blood
- Globulin – a protein found in the blood
- Alkaline Phosphatase – screens for liver and/or muscle and bone health
- Cholesterol – measures the amount of cholesterol in the pet's body
- Total bilirubin – screens for liver and gall bladder and red blood cell health
- Phosphorus – measures the level of phosphorous in the pet's blood
- Amylase – screens for pancreatic health
- Lipase – screens for pancreatic health

ELECTROLYTES

Electrolytes are dissolved chemicals with electrical charge found in the liquid part of the blood. Electrolytes are important for the health of the pet and are involved in many aspects of body function—including the heart, and muscle, and nerve action.

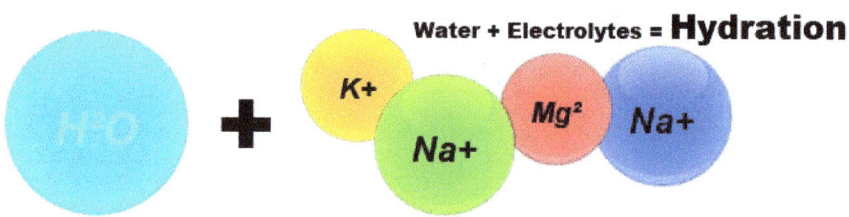

Some electrolytes are:

- sodium
- chloride
- potassium
- calcium
- magnesium
- and many others

PANCREAS TESTS

The pancreas is an organ that has many jobs, one of which is to help break down food.

The pancreas makes enzymes that break down proteins, sugars, and fats to very small particles that can be absorbed and used by the body. If the pancreas is irritated—usually by fatty foods—then it becomes painful and pancreatitis occurs. Pets with pancreatitis may have the following signs:

- pain in the abdomen
- vomiting
- diarrhea with blood sometimes
- lack of appetite
- depression
- or other signs

CPL – (Canine pancreatic lipase) is a separate and special test specifically to identify pancreatitis.

Pancreatitis is a very serious condition and treatment is always recommended.

THYROID TESTS

Thyroid glands are glands located along both sides of the windpipe (trachea) in the neck of the dog.

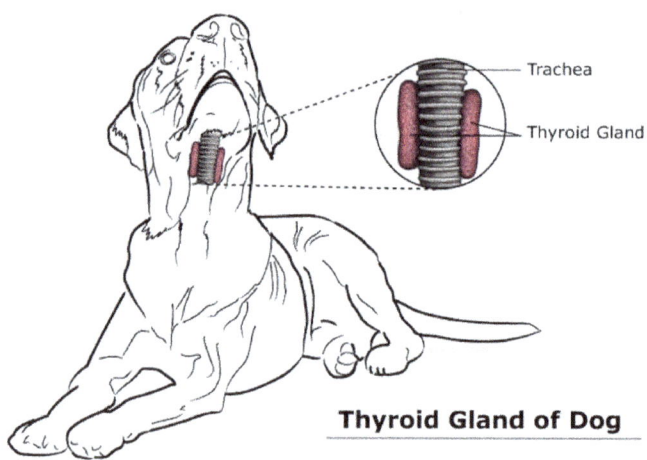

Thyroid Gland of Dog

Thyroid glands make thyroid hormone - a hormone essential for the dog's health.

While cats may have disorders with too much thyroid hormone being made, dogs generally have disorders where too little thyroid hormone is made by their thyroid glands. This is called hypothyroidism (hypo—low; thyroidism— relating to the thyroid).

Some signs of decreased thyroid hormone disorder in the dog include:

- low energy levels—sluggish pets
- decreased interest in playing
- increased sleeping times
- depression
- panting
- staying close to warm places
- overweight
- frequent infection of the ears and/or skin
- thinning hair with bald spots
- slow regrowth of hair
- dry skin with flaking dandruff, or greasy skin
- excessive shedding
- dull hair coat
- high cholesterol

Testing for Thyroid Disorders

Several tests are available for evaluating thyroid disorders; however, the Total Thyroxine—T4—is the level most commonly evaluated.

When T4 levels are low, daily administration of medication is required to replace this hormone.

Pets being given thyroid hormone replacement medication require regular evaluations of the levels of T4 to assure the levels are within the normal range for evaluation of therapy.

Also, the levels determine if the T4 becomes too high with treatment—requiring a decrease in medication given.

The goal of therapy is to maintain the level of T4 hormone in a "normal" range. Testing makes this possible.

BILE ACIDS

When lab tests demonstrate elevations in chemicals (enzymes) made by the liver, veterinarians may recommend bile acids to screen for general liver health and function.

Bile acids are made when pets eat a meal. They help break down food so it can be absorbed. Normally bile acids are reabsorbed; when they are not, they elevate in the blood, are detected on a blood test, and indicate a disorder may be affecting the liver.

Testing for bile acids is simple and involves fasting the pet (not allowing the pet to eat prior to the test), taking a blood sample to measure bile acids, feeding the pet a small amount of food, then taking another blood sample hours afterwards to measure bile acids and evaluate the blood levels.

If the bile acids testing indicates a disorder of the liver, additional testing is recommended to find a cause for the abnormality.

CUSHING'S AND ADDISON'S TESTING

There are many glands in the body that make hormones. We have already discussed the thyroid gland; now we will discuss the adrenal glands.

Adrenal glands are two small glands located just above each kidney. They make hormones necessary for the health of the pet.

Veterinarians evaluate two disorders of these glands—Cushing's and Addison's.

Cushing's (hyper- adrenocorticism—hyper for high; adreno for the adrenals; corticism for coritsol hormone)—this is a condition in which TOO MUCH hormone is made by the glands.

Some signs of Cushing's include:

- increased thirst and urination
- increased hunger
- increased panting
- pot-bellied abdomen
- obesity
- fat pads on the neck and shoulders
- loss of hair
- lack of energy
- inability to sleep (insomnia)
- muscle weakness
- lack of heat cycle in female dogs (anestrus)
- shrinking of testicles
- darkening of the skin
- appearance of blackheads on the skin
- thin skin (from weight gain)
- bruising (from thin, weakened skin)
- hard white scaly patches on the skin, elbows, etc. (associated with the disease calcinosis cutis)

Addison's (hypo- adrenocorticism—hypo for low; adreno for the adrenal; corticism for the cortisol hormone)—this is a condition in which TOO LITTLE hormone is made by the glands.

Some signs of Addison's include:

- listlessness
- loss of appetite
- weight loss
- vomiting
- diarrhea
- shaking
- depression
- dehydration
- weak pulse
- muscle weakness
- collapse
- low body temperature
- blood in feces

Several tests are available for testing Cushing's and Addison's.

Both disorders require close monitoring.

Check with your veterinarian for their recommendations on testing, treatments, and frequent follow-up care for these two disorders.

BLOOD CLOTTING TESTING

It is essential that under the necessary conditions, blood clots. If blood clots too easily, disorders can result; and as well, if blood is not able to clot, loss of life due to bleeding can occur.

Blood clotting is a complicated and complex process that can be measured. The measurement for blood clotting is done by collecting blood in special tubes and having the blood tested for the time it takes for the blood to clot. Clotting times are measured in seconds.

TWO COMMON TESTS TO TEST THE DOG'S ABILITY TO CLOT BLOOD ARE:

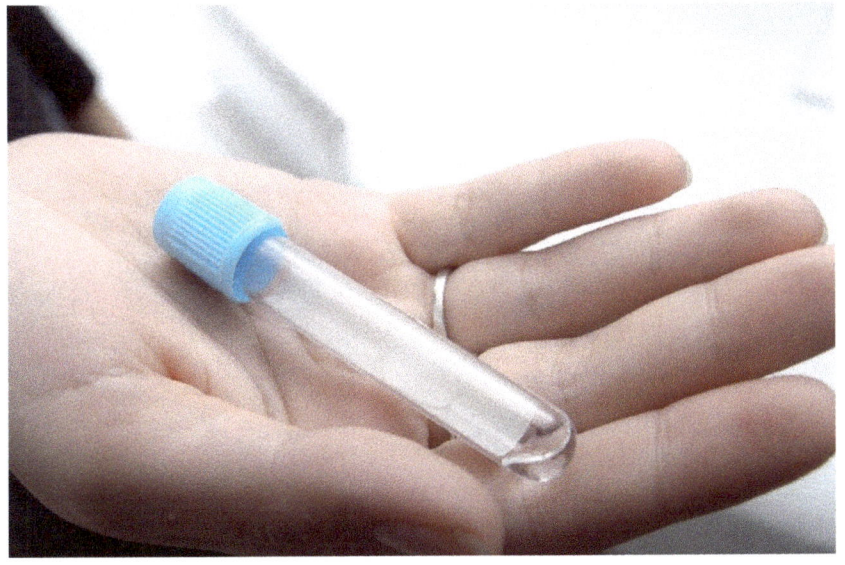

PT – the prothrombin time – measures the time it takes blood to clot.

PTT – the partial thromboplastin time – also measures the time it takes blood to clot.

Conditions that interfere with a dog's ability to clot blood are:

- pet's ingesting poisons—including certain rat/mouse poisons
- certain snake bites
- disorders of the liver
- tick diseases
- medications
- birth disorders such as hemophilia (von Willebrands in Dobermans)

and less likely:

- anemia
- plant or other poisons
- cancer
- long standing infections
- vitamin K deficiencies

If a dog's blood is unable to clot, his/her life is in danger and requires immediate care.

Some signs of bleeding or abnormalities in a pet's ability to clot include:

- nosebleeds for no apparent reason
- bleeding in the urine
- bleeding in the stool
- bleeding gums
- bruising of the skin of the belly or legs
- swollen joints
- pale gums if bleeding has been prolonged
- a wound not stopping bleeding within a reasonable time

DIABETIC TESTING

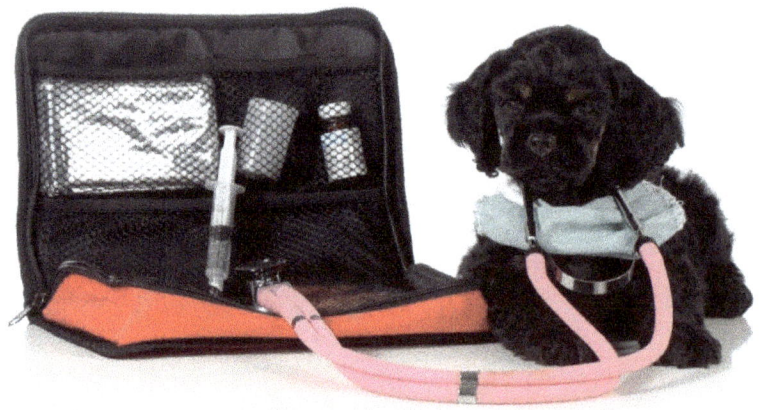

Diabetes mellitus is a disorder of a dog's ability to properly use sugar.

Most dogs with diabetes require insulin daily.

Dogs also require a special diet to assist in controlling their blood sugars.

Dogs require close monitoring of the effects of the insulin as well.

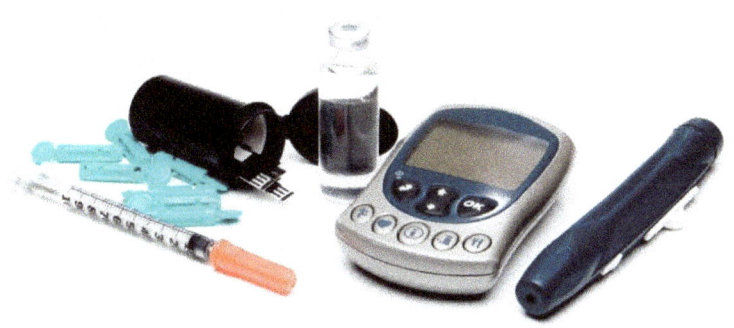

Accucheck is a test with a small machine that uses one drop of blood to quickly measure the sugar (glucose) in the blood.

Blood glucose is a test in a veterinarian office or a laboratory to test for the level of sugar (glucose) in the pet's blood. A larger amount of blood is required to complete this test.

Glucose curve is a series of sugar (glucose) measurements after a pet is given insulin. This testing is useful in adjusting the dosage of medication (insulin) being given to a diabetic pet.

Fructosamine is a measurement of the sugar in a pet's blood over a long period of time. This test is useful in evaluating the effective use of insulin in treating diabetes.

X-RAYS

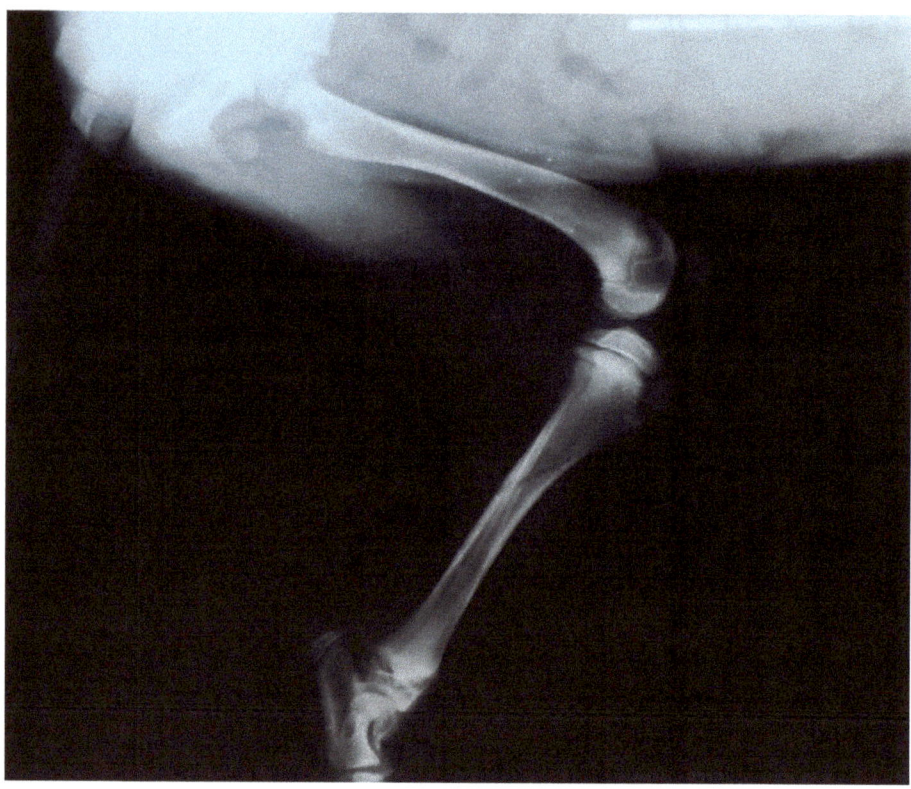

Radiographs—AKA x-rays—are useful in identifying broken bones, arthritis, obstructions in a pet's intestines, heart size, enlarged organs, stones in bladders, screening lung health, and sometimes other uses.

ULTRASOUND

Ultrasound is a non-invasive test without radiation, available for more detailed imaging of body organs such as the heart, liver, kidneys, pancreas, eyes, lymph nodes, testicles, ovaries and uterus, unborn puppies, intestines, spleen, stones in bladders, and so forth.

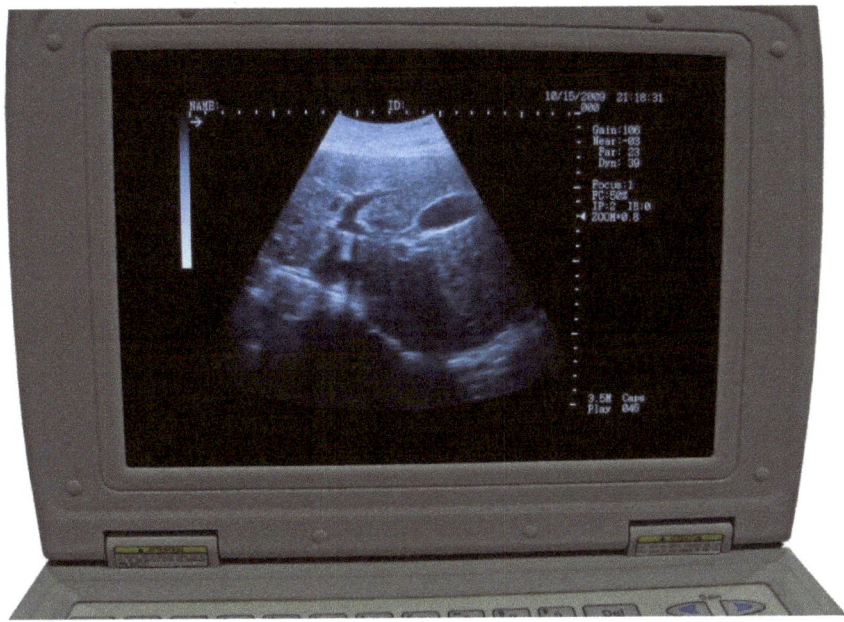

Some veterinarians are skilled at this technique and some advise referral to specialists for this testing.

ADVANCED IMAGING

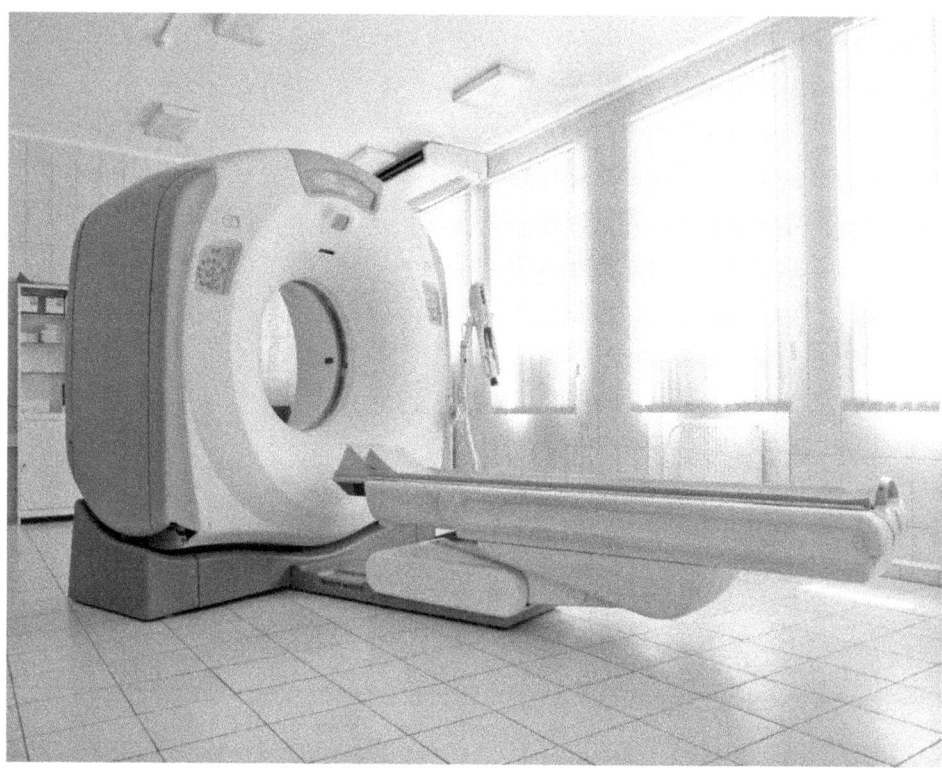

More advanced imaging has been developed. This includes the CT scan (computerized topography) and the MRI (magnetic resonance imaging). These tests are more accurate and quicker at helping veterinarians find and treat disorders affecting dogs.

SKIN TESTING

Owners frequently present with concerns about skin that include:

- itching and scratching
- scooting
- thickening of the skin
- darkening of the skin color
- flaking
- excessive licking of legs/paws / any body area
- hair loss
- rash
- open bleeding areas on the skin
- growths in the skin
- odor to the skin
- weeping skin
- oily skin
- fleas
- and other symptoms

SKIN DISORDERS

POSSIBLE DISORDERS OF THE SKIN INCLUDE:

1. **Immune**-mediated diseases – which includes skin allergies to grasses, pollens, and molds as well as other allergens
2. **Physical/environmental conditions** – which include "hot spots," lick irritations
3. **Infections** – with any bacteria or yeast- one example is staph, a normal bacteria found on the skin, and another is malassezia, a normal fungi (yeast) found on the skin; also included are mites listed below—Demodex and Sarcoptes
4. **Ringworm** – is also considered an infectious condition of the skin, caused by a fungi that grows on the skin
5. **Fleas and ticks** – may be seen on the skin of dogs and puppies
6. **Hereditary conditions** – which includes seborrhea (too much oil made by the skin), psoriasis (too little oil is made by the skin) pattern baldness, and color dilution to name a few
7. **Symptoms** of skin disease can be related to conditions occurring inside the body, such as a low-functioning thyroid or high-functioning adrenal glands as discussed before
8. **Tumors** cancers in the skin area

…**just to name a few** conditions veterinarians must consider when presented with skin concerns.

Skin tests include:

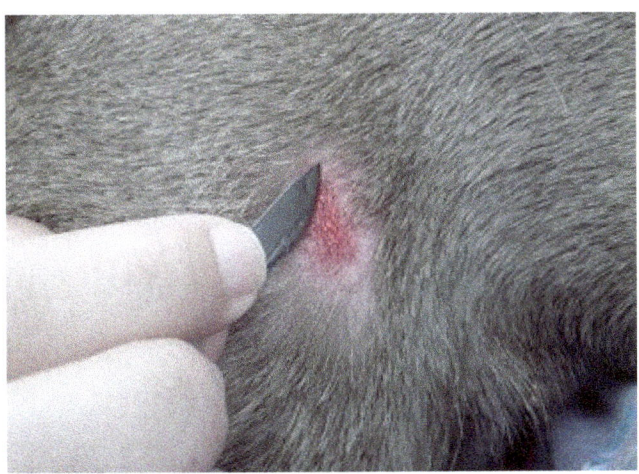

- skin scraping
- skin biopsy
- fine needle aspirate
- skin impressions
- cultures of the skin

Skin is easy to test because it is accessible to a veterinarian.

SKIN SCRAPING

A skin scrape is where a sharp blade is used to scrape affected areas of skin to place on a microscope slide to view the scraping under the microscope.

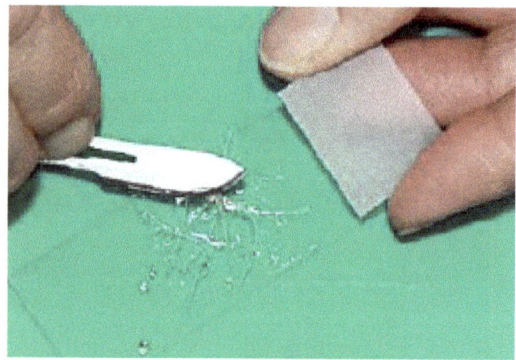

Veterinarians usually recommend skin scraping to detect Demodex or Sarcoptic mites.

DEMODEX (MANGE)

Demodex (demodecosis) is a skin disorder where mites that look similar to cigars live in hair follicles.

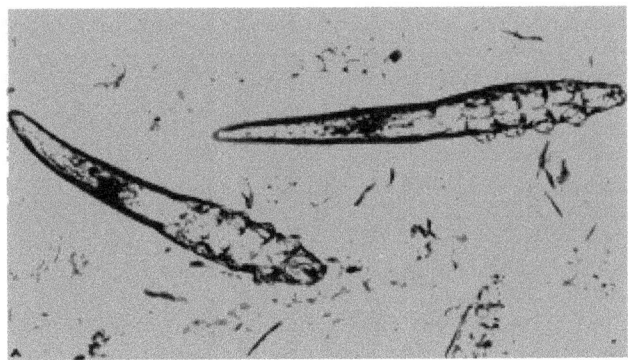

Some signs of Demodex include:

1. hair loss on any area of a dog's body
2. itching and scratching
3. reddening of the skin
4. sores
5. dry skin
6. and scales
7. if severe, the pet may be depressed

Any age pet can be affected, but usually young puppies present to the veterinarian with Demodex mites.

Several treatments are available to treat this mite.

SARCOPTIC MANGE

Sarcoptic mites are mites that burrow into the skin of affected pets.

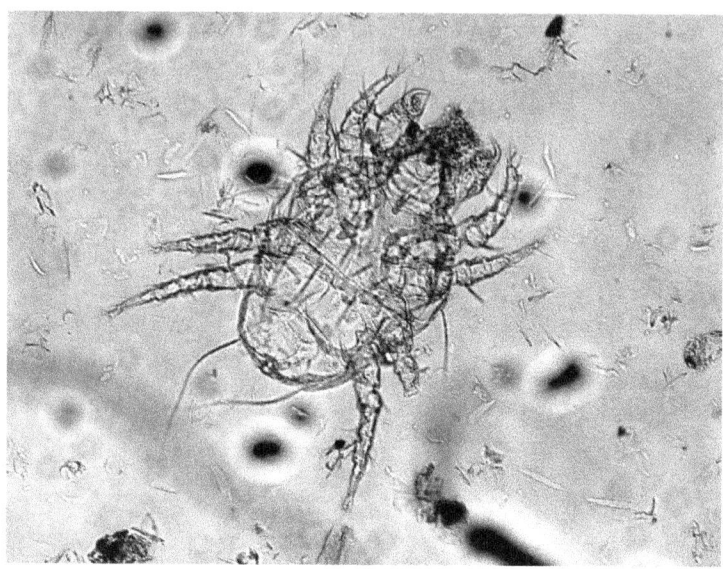

Some signs of Sarcoptic mites include:

1. intense itching and scratching
2. hair loss that can be extreme
3. red bumps
4. red skin, open sores
5. depression
6. loss of appetite due to being so uncomfortable, resulting in…
7. weight loss

If owners are in close contact with an infected pet, they may be at risk for these mites to burrow in their skin and cause intense itching, however, humans are considered a temporary host for the mite.

Several treatments are available to treat Sarcoptes.

FINE NEEDLE ASPIRATION AND BIOPSY

Growths (tumors) are common in pets.

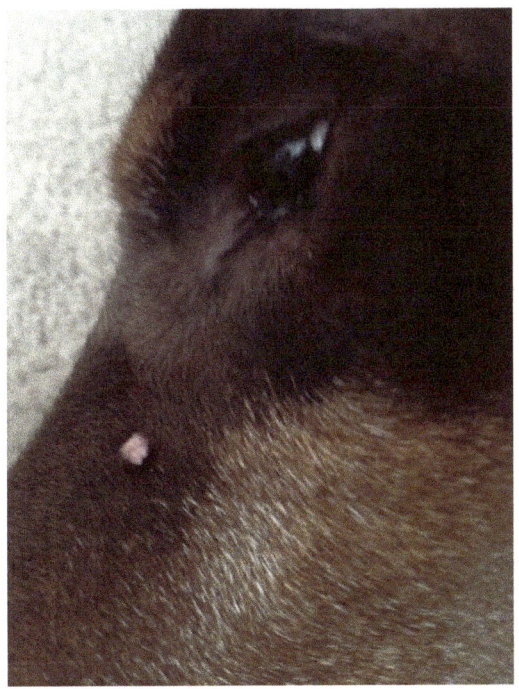

Growths can be in the skin, muscle, bone, liver, spleen, heart—every area of the body!

The two types of growths are:
- harmless—just needs to be removed without spread to other body places
- harmful—spreads or regrows in the original place

Testing of growths includes **FNA and biopsy:**

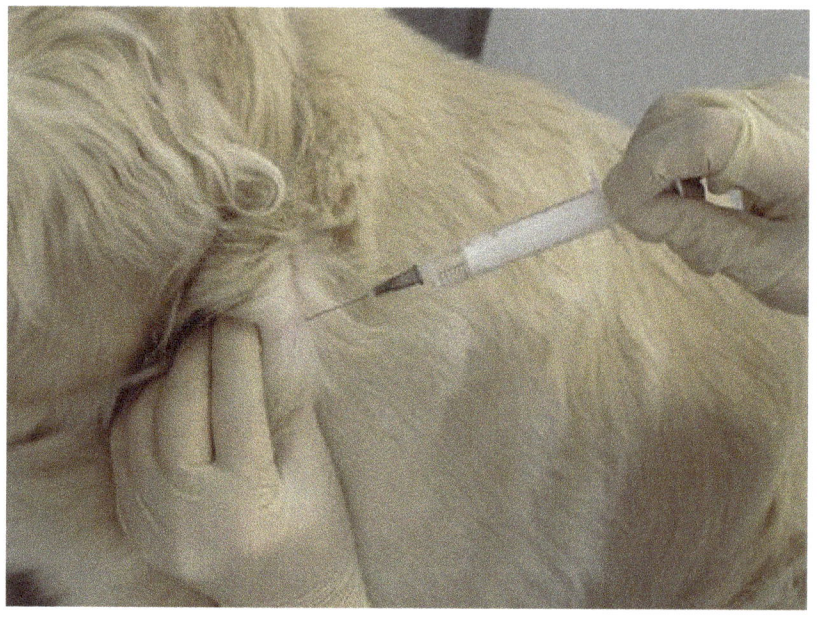

FNA – fine needle aspirate – a simple test in which a needle is inserted into a growth, small parts of it are collected in the needle; the parts are placed on a glass slide, sent to the lab, and read by specialists to decide the source and behavior of the growth —and if it is harmless or harmful.

Biopsy – a test in which a section of or the entire growth is removed and sent to the specialists to examine to decide the source and behavior of the growth—and if it is harmless or harmful to the pet.

ALLERGIES

An allergy is when a pet has a localized or generalized reaction after exposure to an internal or external substance the pet is allergic to.

Some types of allergies in dogs are:

1. fleas
2. food
3. contact with chemicals and other substances
4. bacterial hypersensitivity
5. insect bites
6. dust and house dust mites
7. inhalant (spores and pollens)
8. vaccines
9. and medication allergies

ALLERGY TESTNG

Testing is required to identify the source of an allergy, because most of the signs of allergy are the skin signs listed on the page before and are the same for almost all allergies.

Allergy testing can be:

- **skin testing** – in which a skin specialist shaves hair from the pet, injects different allergens into the skin of the pet, and observes if a reaction occurs in the skin

- **blood testing** – in which a blood sample is collected, sent to the lab, and tested for allergies

Testing is recommended when the allergic signs are at their worst.

After specific allergies are identified, treatment is recommended. This treatment may include flea medication, changes in food, or immunotherapy.

IMMUNOTHERAPY

Immunotherapy is specially formulated medication that is given to an allergic pet to decrease and/or eliminate a pet's response when exposed to a substance they are allergic to.

Immunotherapy can be in the form of injections the pet receives or in the form of liquid drops that are placed into the pet's mouth.

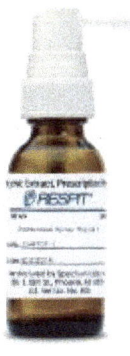

Oromucosal Spray 30 ml multidose bottles (14–21 week supply)

This therapy decreases or eliminates the need for other medications to treat the signs of skin irritation.

Allergies cannot be cured; however, they can be managed to improve the quality of life for a pet.

FLEAS

Many pets have fleas in their fur; however, some dogs have a reaction to them. These pets have a flea allergy. Signs of flea allergy are the same signs listed for general allergies.

Recommended treatment for fleas includes:

- treating all pets in the home all year
- cleaning all surfaces and bedding related to the pet
- treating the environment if possible

Pets allergic to fleas may require additional medication to ease the intense itching and scratching they experience when exposed to fleas.

FOOD ALLERGY

Pets can be allergic to the meat, grains, additives, or any ingredient in their food.

Testing is available to identify food allergies as well as food trials are implemented to assist in identifying food allergies.

Signs of food allergies are the same as listed earlier for general allergies, however, signs may also include vomiting and/or diarrhea.

Several pet foods are available for potential food allergies.

CONTACT ALLERGIES

Lawn chemicals, cleaning solutions, fabrics (such as wool and nylon), salts used for ice and snow, and many other items that come in direct contact with skin can cause allergic reactions.

Identifying potential sources of contact allergies is important because it is usually simple to eliminate exposure to the allergy-producing source to make the pet comfortable.

BACTERIAL HYPERSENSITIVITY

Staph (staphylococcus) bacteria is a normal bacteria found on the surface of pet's skin; however, some dogs have a sensitivity to this bacteria, which results in skin irritation and sores—an allergic reaction.

Several treatments are available for this hypersensitivity (allergy).

INSECT BITES

Some signs of insect bite allergy include:

1. redness
2. swelling
3. itching and scratching
4. swelling
5. hives

Treatment is available for insect bite irritation and allergy.

INHALANT ALLERGIES (ATOPY)

This type of allergy is suspected after all others have been eliminated as the cause of a pet's skin irritation. Inhalant allergies occur when a dog is exposed to airborne respiratory irritants. Skin irritation is noted as a sign of an inhalant allergy.

This is the largest area of allergy-related disorders in dogs. It includes:

- animal dander
- airborne pollens—grasses, weeds, trees, etc.
- house dust and dust mites

Since some inhalant allergies relate to spores and pollens in the air as plants bloom and blossom in nature, the signs of allergy may only occur during the common sporing time for the offending plants.

Some inhalant allergies are constant because the exposure is constant—such as with house dust and dust mites.

Some signs of inhalant allergies include:

- intense itching and scratching
- licking areas of the skin
- recurrent ear infections
- mutilating the skin
- hair loss
- redness to the skin
- dry skin
- flaking skin
- infections with itching and scratching

Areas of skin irritation can be anywhere; however, common sites are:

- the ears
- the front and back leg joints
- the face
- under the front legs
- in the groin areas
- around the eyes
- between the digits of the paws

If a pet has an inhalant allergy, wiping pets off with a damp cloth after being on grass is beneficial in decreasing the signs of allergies. It is important to wipe the feet, the body, and the head of the pet.

Testing recommended is the skin and/or blood testing discussed in earlier sections.

The ideal treatment for allergies is to identify the allergy and give immunotherapy specifically against that allergy.

VACCINE AND MEDICATION REACTIONS

On occasion reactions occur after vaccines have been administered.

These allergies were addressed in chapter 3.

MEDICATION REACTIONS

Avoidance of medications that cause adverse reactions in pets is recommended.

CULTURES

Cultures are samples taken of fluids or tissues that are then placed on special gel plates so bacteria or fungi can grow and be identified.

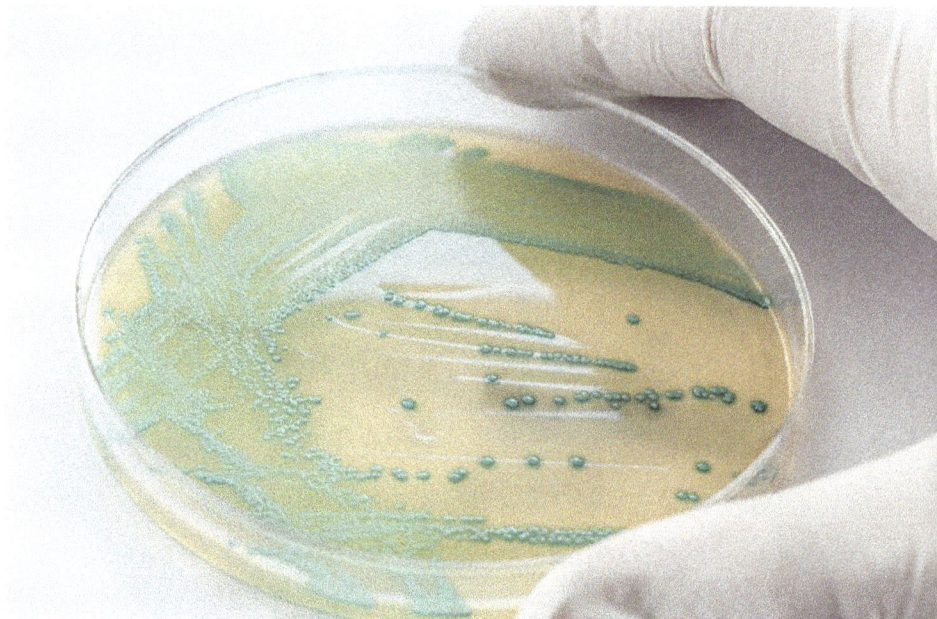

Fluids commonly cultured are:

- blood
- urine
- wound fluids
- skin
- ears

Cultures are usually recommended when infections are severe or are not improving with treatment.

FUNGAL CULTURES

DTM (dermatophyte test media) is a special culture gel used to detect fungal infections.

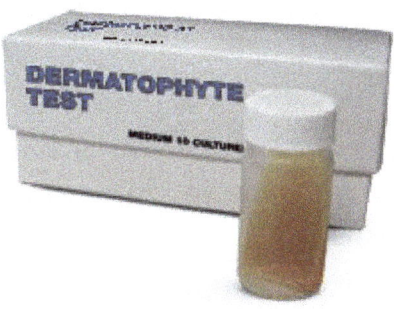

Ringworm is not a worm but is the most common fungal infection of the skin. Ringworm is not a worm at all and can grow on any part of the skin; however, it is mostly seen on the face and the legs. The areas infected are usually circular (ring-like).

Ringworm is a threat to people because they can acquire ringworm when exposed to dogs with the infection.

URINE EXAMS

Owners frequently present pets to veterinarians for concerns relating to urinary disorders in dogs that include:

1. blood in urine—sometimes seen as "red-tinged" urine
2. inability to urinate—which is an emergency
3. urinating frequently
4. urinating small amounts of urine
5. urinating large amounts of urine
6. urine with a strong or foul odor
7. seeing stones passed in urine
8. crying with pain

DISORDERS OF THE URINARY SYSTEM

Some disorders of the urinary system in dogs include:

1. infection
2. diseases such as diabetes or liver or other organ disorders
3. tumors
4. stones (calculi)
5. crystals—several different types may be found

URINE TESTING

Urine exam—the urinalysis—is recommended when owners have concerns or as a routine screening test.

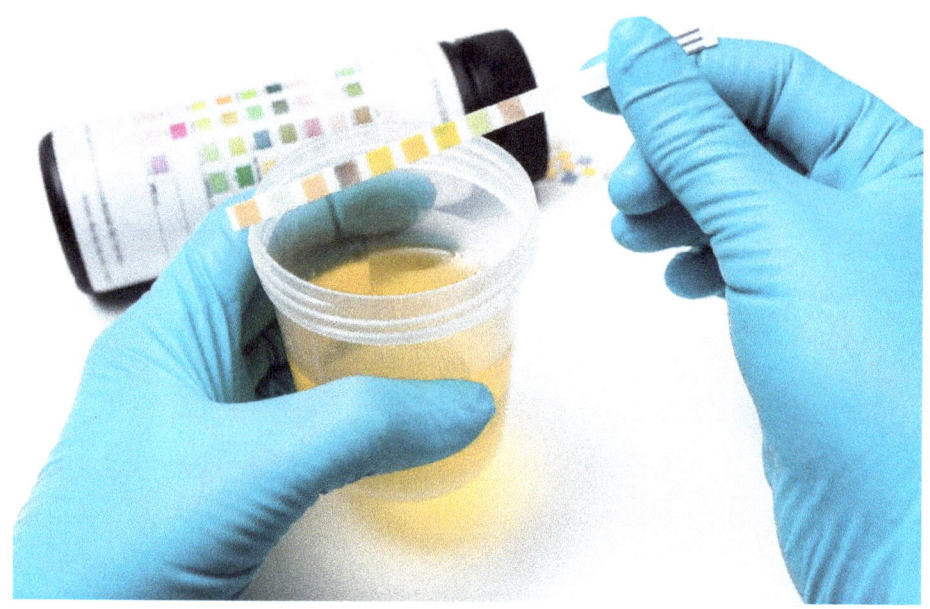

The 3 parts to a urine exam are:

1. specific gravity—measures urine concentration
2. the "strip" portion—screens for protein, blood, white blood cells, sugar, and other items in the urine
3. the "microscopic" portion—examines stained slides for crystals, red and white blood cells, tumor cells, and other potential findings.

SIGNS OF EAR DISORDERS

Owners frequent seek veterinarian care for concerns regarding a pet's ear or ears that include:

1. scratching or rubbing the ears
2. crying when the ears are touched or massaged
3. odor from the ears
4. discharge from the ears—brown, green, or yellow
5. tilting of the pet's head
6. circling
7. loss of balance
8. sores to the ear flap
9. shaking their head
10. hair loss around the ear
11. swelling or redness to the ears
12. and possibly hearing loss

EAR EXAMS

Veterinarians examine a dog's ear canal and ear drum with an oto - (ear) scope.

When discharge is present in the ears of a dog, an ear swab exam may be recommended.

Ear swabs help direct the care recommended for ear disorders and are completed by…

- using a Q-tip to obtain a sample of the ear discharge from the ear canals
- this discharge is placed on a slide
- then stained
- then examined for yeast and bacteria

EAR CARE

For ear health, veterinarians recommend:

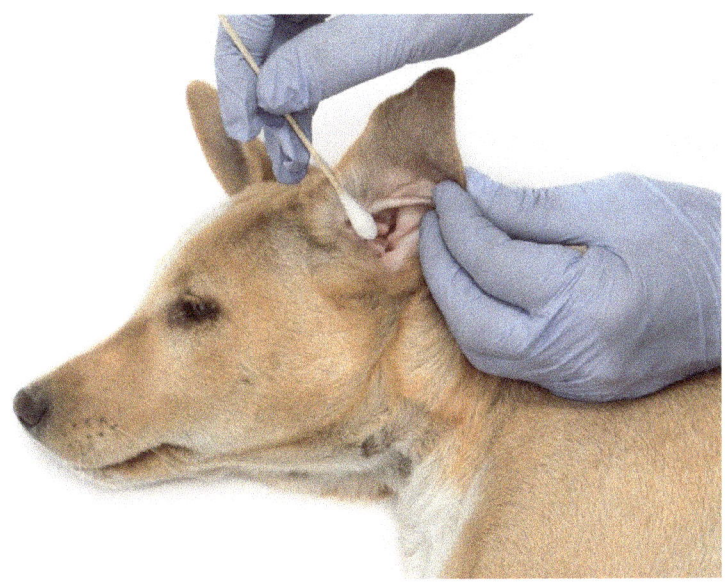

1. removal of all ear hair inside the canals
2. cleaning the ears if there is discharge
3. using medication recommended by your veterinarian
4. cleaning the ears after bathing and swimming
5. trimming all unnecessary hair from the ear flap to lighten the flap and allow air to circulate—as for spaniels with heavily haired ears
6. treating all known diseases—such as allergies/diabetes/others
7. having the ears checked regularly

SIGNS OF EYE DISORDERS

Owners frequently present pets to veterinarians for concerns relating to a pet's eye or eyes that include:

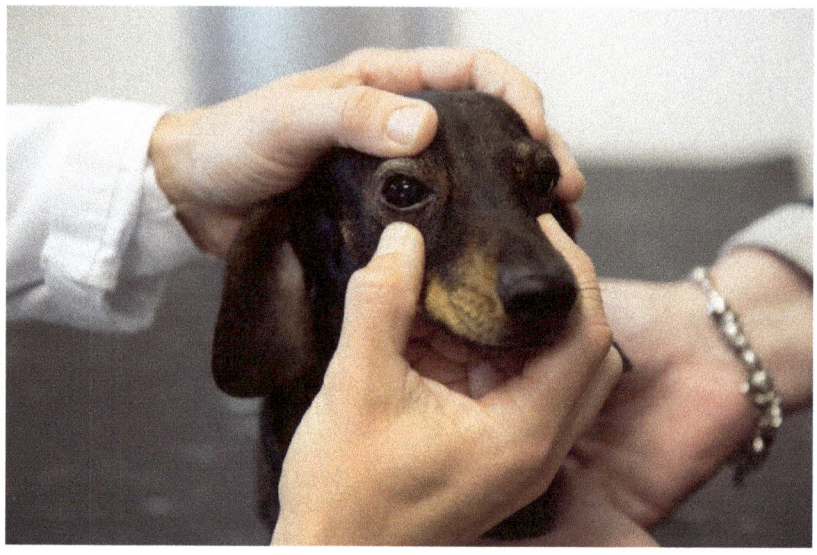

1. excessive tearing
2. squinting
3. swelling
4. eyelashes that point into the eyes
5. eyelids that roll into the eye
6. eyelids that roll away from the eye
7. pigment on the surface of the eye
8. reddening of the eyelids
9. cloudiness inside or on the surface of the eye
10. colored discharge (white, tan, green, yellow) around the eye
11. pain
12. unequal pupil size
13. bleeding from the eye or inside the eye
14. "cherry" eye (a pink mass noted at the inner corner of the eye
15. injury to the eye—from being hit, bitten, scratched
16. inability to see

DISORDERS OF THE EYE

Disorders of the eyes in dogs include:

- infections
- disorders of the cornea (the clear surface of the eye)
- disorders of the lens (including cataracts)
- cherry eye
- foreign objects in the eye
- cuts to the eye or eyelids
- trauma- an injury to the eye
- proptosis (eyes popping out)
- tumors
- disorders of the eyelids

- pannus (pigmentation on the surface of the eye)
- blindness
- glaucoma
- and more

EYE EXAMINATION

Veterinarians examine the dog's eye with an ophthalmoscope—to visualize deep and superficial areas of the eye.

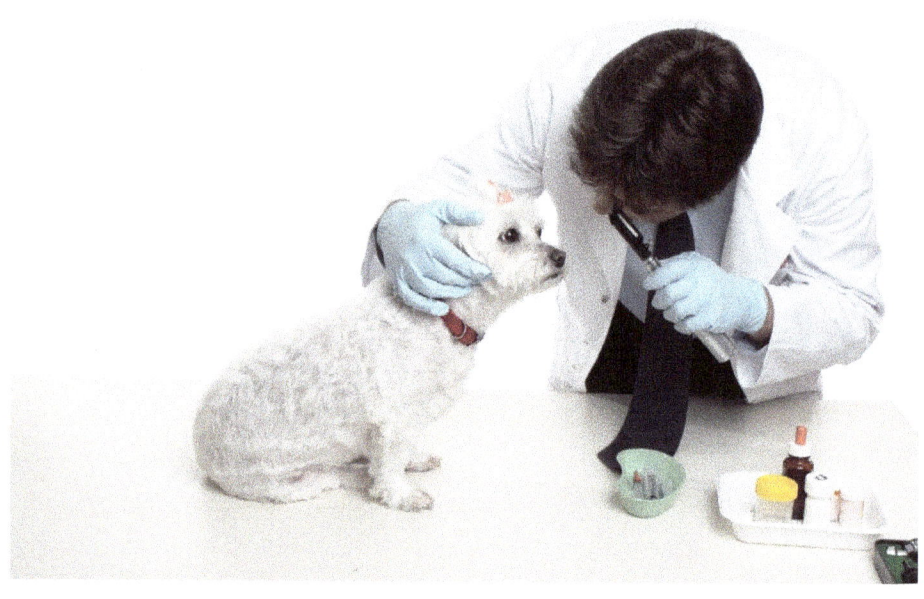

Specialists are available for severe disorders of the eye.

Three tests common in evaluating pets' eyes are:

STAINING TESTS FOR THE EYE

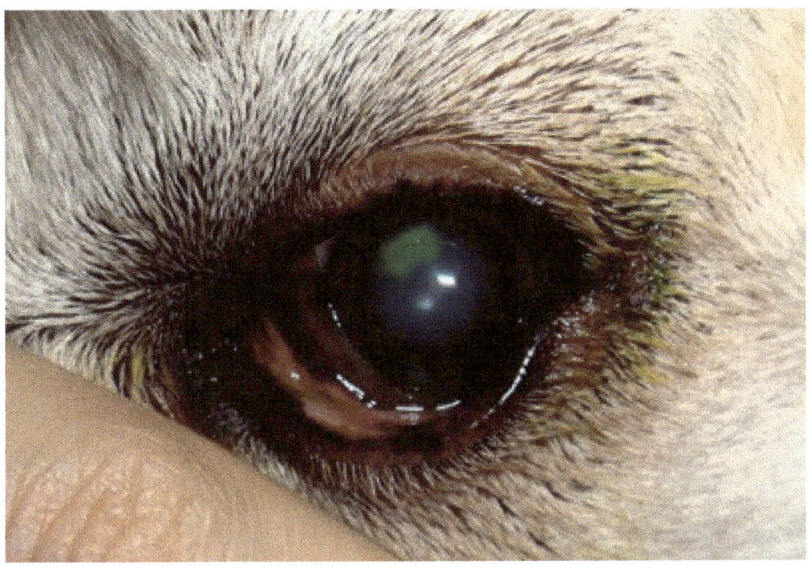

Fluorescein stain – a liquid green dye applied to the surface of the eye to detect superficial defects on the surface of the eye. If a defect is present, the stain will dye this area a green color.

TEAR TESTING FOR THE EYE

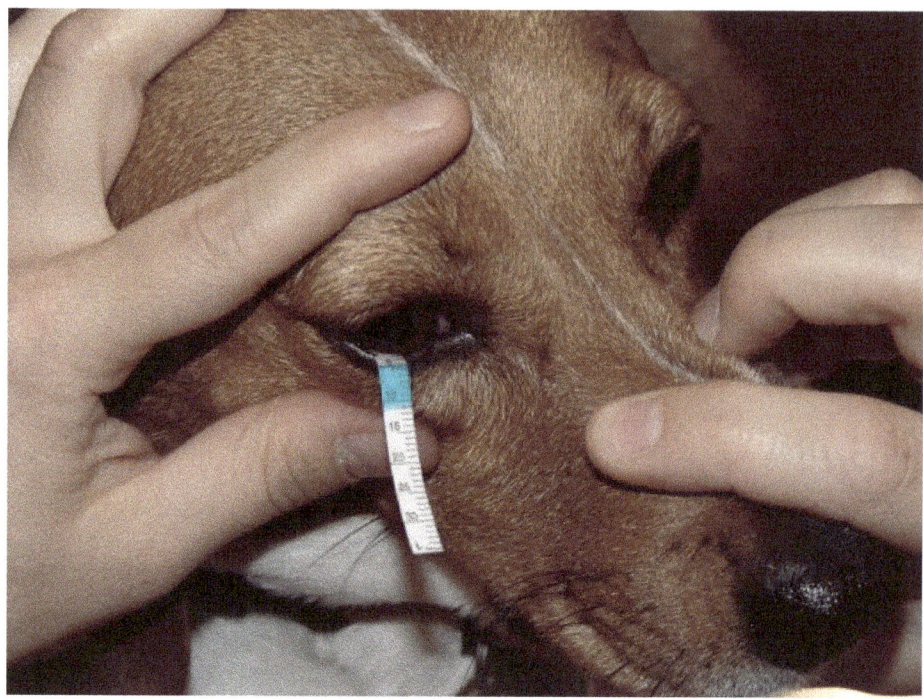

Tear testing – in which a small piece of special paper with measurement lines is inserted into the lower eyelid for one minute and the amount of liquid tears present on the paper is measured.
Healthy eyes constantly make tears that are spread over the eyes each time a pet blinks. Tears keep the eyes moist and clean.

When too many tears are made, they spill over onto the fur of the face—a condition called epiphora.

When there are too little tears made, a disorder that is called "dry eye" occurs- this is called keratoconjunctivitis sicca. This condition requires lifelong treatment to keep the affected eyes healthy.

TONOMETRY

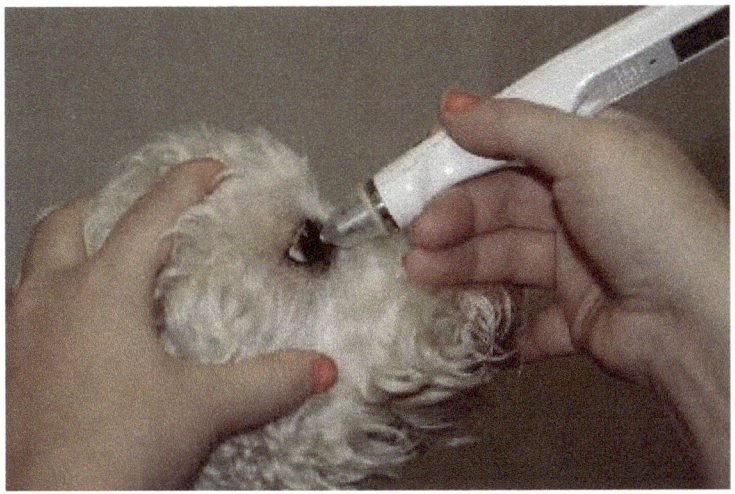

A tonometer- or tono pen – as seen above, measures the pressure in the eye.

This test screens for glaucoma. Glaucoma is an eye disorder that is present when eye pressures are high (elevated). Glaucoma can be very painful and can cause loss of vision. This test will help determine if a dog requires treatment for this condition.

The **BENEFITS** of testing are that it allows veterinarians the best practice options…

… to keep pets healthy and happy.

Chapter 13

MISCELLANEOUS

LOST PETS

Many owners find themselves in the unfortunate position of having lost a pet.

- every few seconds a lost pet is taken to an animal shelter
- we want you to be one of the lucky families reunited with their lost pet

TIPS FOR FINDING LOST PETS

Some helpful recommendations for finding a lost pet are:

- **Act immediately** – the quicker a search is started, the more likely the lost pet may be found
- **Utilize web sources** – there are several on line sources for posting or checking for lost pets
- **Check local pet shelters** – know all the local shelters in your immediate area and several surrounding areas—it is possible for pets to travel distances when lost
- **Contact animal control agencies** – know all the local authorities and their policies regarding lost pets
- **Call local papers** – some papers have special areas in the paper to post about lost and/or found pets
- **Call micro chipping services-** if your pet is micro chipped, call to ask if their are any lost animals reported found, and also advise them of your lost pet

(Additional tips for findings lost pets)

- **Look everywhere** – in your neighborhood and in surrounding neighborhoods
- **Visit local businesses** – they may allow you to post signs, or someone may have seen the pet while coming to work
- **Talk to letter carriers** – they are in the neighborhood and can keep an eye out or may have seen your pet
- **Talk to neighbors**
- **Talk to the paper delivery person**
- **Talk to the garbage collector**
- **Ask children in the neighborhood**
- **Advertise** a reward; however, consider not posting the amount of the reward
- **Post signs** up in neighborhood
- **Microchip** your pet
- **Attach** a name tag and phone number to a collar of your pet
- **Do not give up**

MICROCHIPPING

Micro chipping is a small cylinder (about the size of a grain of rice) that is injected beneath a pet's skin—usually in the area between the shoulders. With active pets, the chip may move slightly from the original site of insertion.

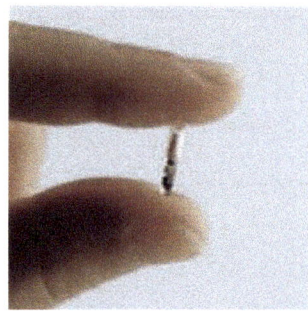

Each cylinder has a number that is unique and identifies the pet it is inserted into.

The chips are scanned with a special scanner that connects information to owners.

There are national and international chips available if you plan to travel abroad with a pet.

EMERGENCIES

Emergencies happen to pets. Being prepared helps during these stressful times.

Common pet emergencies include:
- being hit by a car
- poisoning
- twisting of the stomach (something that happens mainly to larger dogs)
- broken bones
- objects stuck in the intestine (shoes, rocks, clothing, etc.)
- overheating in automobiles or in warm environments
- low body temperature if out in cold environments
- snake bite
- being unable to urinate
- other animal bites
- bleeding from any body area
- eye injuries
- limping
- vomiting
- reactions to vaccines or medications
- seizures (particularly if they do not stop, or if the pet has several in succession)
- sudden collapse
- any sudden change in a pet's condition

WHAT TO DO IN AN EMERGENCY

- be prepared.
- know any dangers in the world around you—weather, snakes, plants, animals, and more.
- begin transferring the pet to a veterinary clinic as soon as possible.
- while seeking veterinary care, have someone drive you if possible.

CHECKING A PET'S TEMPERATURE, HEART RATE AND BREATHING RATE

HERE'S HOW:

Check Vital Signs—
Heart Rate, Breathing (respiratory) Rate, Temperature

Heart rate – 60–140 beats per minute is normal; pain and fear may make the rate higher
To check the pet's heart rate, place a hand over the chest; another way to check a pulse is to slip your hand under rear leg into the groin to feel a pulse (owners can be shown); measure for 15 seconds and multiply x 4

Breathing (respiratory) rate – 15–34 breaths per minute are normal; pain and fear may make the rate higher. To check the pet's respiratory rate, observe chest rising and, if you know how, listen with a stethoscope (owners can be shown); measure for 15 seconds and multiply x 4

Temperature – 100–102.5 F. To check the temperature, always use a rectal digital thermometer

Abnormal temperatures are if < 100 F or > 103 F

Never be afraid to ask someone to show you how to check your pet.

Seek veterinary care immediately and...

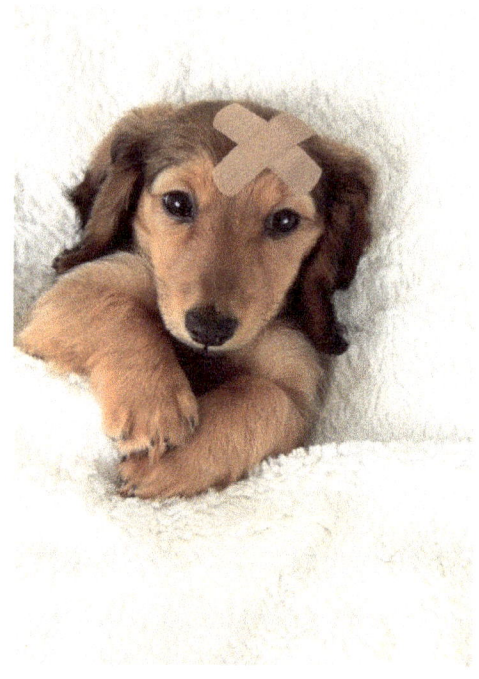

- STAY CALM
- do not put your face or a child's face by the injured pet's face—they may bite if fearful or painful even if they would not under normal circumstances
- muzzle an injured pet if necessary for safety—you may use gauze or cloth strips made from a soft towel or cloth, or purchase a muzzle for your emergency kit
- if the pet is overheated, begin to cool pet off by placing the pet in a shaded area with a fan - if t > 104, seek a vet immediately and use tepid water baths and apply isopropyl rubbing alcohol to the pet's foot pads—this may help lower the temperature
- wrap cold pets in warm blankets—but do not rub areas that may be frostbitten
- wrap injured small pups in towels for transport

ALSO:

- do not drag a large injured dog—try to make a stretcher of a rug, large towel, child's sled, or a board
- protect injured legs or broken legs—rescuers can use rolled-up blankets, towels, or newspapers to protect or immobilize an injured leg by placing them next to the injured legs to act as splints or supports—this helps the injured part stay still while the pet is being transported to the veterinary clinic
- pillows may be used to place injured legs on if the leg does not have to be lifted high to the pillow—this pads the injured leg and also helps keep it still while transporting to the veterinary clinic
- take any poisons or medications the pet has ingested
- use soft bandages for open wounds or bleeding—apply gentle pressure to bleeding areas - you may need to keep gentle pressure until the bleeding stops or you arrive at the veterinary clinic

FIRST AID KITS
Items You May Want to Include in a Home First Aid Kit

- alcohol (70% isopropyl alcohol—rubbing alcohol)
- antibacterial cream
- bandaging material—gauze pads, gauze rolls, rolls of cotton, self-adhesive wraps such as "vet wrap" or "co flex" bandage
- cotton balls
- hydrogen peroxide
- rectal thermometer
- scissors
- blankets and towels
- tweezers
- soft muzzles
- the phone numbers to the local emergency clinics
- the phone number to poison control

Keep the kit in a sealed container in your home and/or vehicle.

DOING YOUR OWN PET EXAM

Knowing what a normal exam is for your pet makes it easier to know when veterinary care is needed.

Basic Physical Exam is from head to toe.

First – Before starting an exam, look at your pet in general. Are they awake, happy to see you, moving correctly? Wagging their tail? How are they standing and breathing?

Normal: awake and playful, responding when called, walking correctly, breathing easily
Not Normal: will not wake up for you, unable to stand, breathing heavily

Head *– Look at the pet's head area*

Normal: rounded forehead, smooth hair coat, no missing hair, no bumps
Not Normal: open wounds, bumps or swelling on surface, shape of the head not the same on both sides

Eyes *– Look at both eyes*

Normal: bright, moist, clear, equal pupils, whites of eyes white in color, look the same on both sides, looks at you when you are talking
Not normal: dull, sunken eyes that appear dry or cloudy, colored discharge from the eyes, yellow or red color to the whites of the eyes, squinting, swelling. painful appearance to the eyes, crying when attempting to open the eyelids

Ears *– Look at both ears*

Normal: pale pink, no odor, dry, typical carriage of ears for breed
Not Normal: swelling to any area of the ear, odor, redness, pain, wounds, scabs, rash, not carrying ears the same on both sides—for example, one up, one down

(Continued exam of the areas around the head)

Nose – Look at the nose

Normal: moist and clean
Not Normal: very dry and cracked, colored discharge—white, green, yellow, tan, red, bleeding, swelling, loss of pigment (coloring) of the nose

Throat *– Look at the throat and gently feel the throat as well*

Normal: no cough, no swellings or growths, all areas feel the same on both sides of the neck
Not Normal: cough when gently feeling the neck area, difficulties in breathing, swelling, growths, anything that feels larger on one side than the other

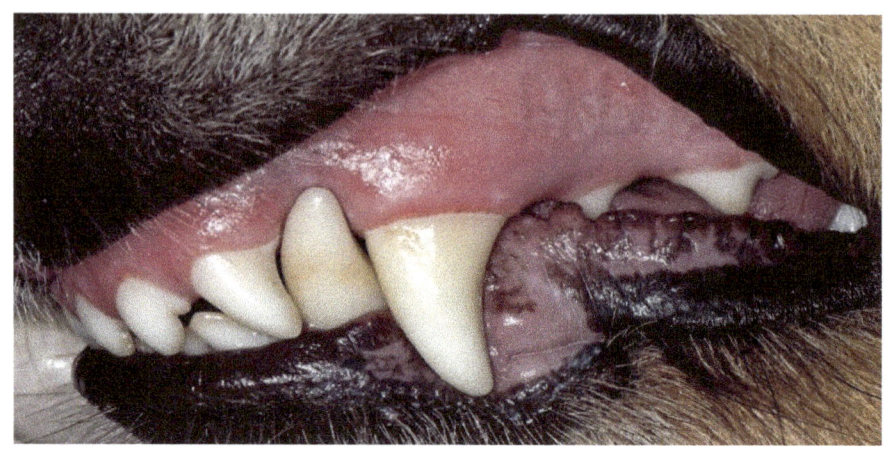

Oral *– look at the pet's teeth and open mouth by turning up the lip fold.*

Normal: teeth are clean and white; the gums are pink and not overgrown
Not Normal: tartar on teeth, recession of gums, reddening of the gums, odor to the mouth or green/tan/yellow discharge from the gums around any teeth, sores in the mouth, growths in the mouth, excess gums over the teeth

MM *– The mucous membranes (AKA the gums)—look at the area under the lip and above the teeth. What color is it?*

Normal: pink
Not Normal: pale pink, cherry red

Capillary refill time (CRT) *– is completed by lifting the upper lip, pressing the gum above the teeth to make the gum pale, and measuring how long it takes to return back to pink. 1–2 seconds is normal*

Heart/Lungs *– Listen for breathing and feel the heart by placing a hand along the side of the pet's chest or placing a hand on the inside of the pet's back leg*

Normal: regular heart rate and easy breathing, even moving of the chest in and out with breathing
Not Normal: any noises heard as pet breaths, irregular, slow or fast heart rate, coughing, any visible signs of difficulty breathing, any blue coloring of the mouth, pet unable to rest or lie down

Abdomen *– Feel the abdomen of the pet by placing your hands just behind the ribs and gently pressing into the abdomen; move slowly and gently from the front of the abdomen to the back of the abdomen*

Normal: soft, not painful, slim (if the pet is not overweight), no lumps, bumps, masses

(Continued exam of the body areas)

Not normal: large, tense, rounded, painful when touching, any lumps, bumps, or masses

Neurological – *Examine the pet's ability to walk properly and respond properly.*

Normal: can feel you touch them, all four paws stand properly on the floor, able to walk in a straight line
Not Normal: head tilting to one side, inability to walk, pain or no pain when pinching paws, seizures, fainting, inability to wake a pet, paws knuckling over

Skin/Coat – *Look at and feel the pet's skin and hair coat*

Normal: shiny, smooth, soft, unbroken hair and smooth skin, minimal odor
Not Normal: sparse or patchy hair coat, open sores or wounds, growths, excess oil in the skin, dry skin, reddening, odor, rash

Extremities – *Look at all 4 legs of the pet*

Normal: able to walk evenly on all 4 legs, no deformities, no growths, no swelling
Not Normal: unable to walk on 1 or more legs, swelling, pain when touching areas, growths, dangling legs, open wounds, odor, discharge of any color

(Continued exam of the skin and extremities)

Lymph nodes *– These may be difficult to locate on a pet unless they are enlarged*

Normal: unable to feel lymph nodes
Not Normal: swelling in the areas of the lymph nodes—under the jaw, in front of the front legs, in front of the back legs, behind the knees, in the groin or under the front legs

Muscles and bones *– Look at the pet's back and legs and muscles over the body*

Normal: muscles soft and covering the bones evenly on both sides of the body part being examined, able to walk without pain
Not Normal: small muscle size in any area, tense muscles, pain when gently feeling over the spine and other body areas, pain when walking, jumping, playing

Urogenital – *Examine the pet's ability to pass urine, and the male and female parts of the pet*

Normal: clean and dry areas—no discharge, swelling, pain
Not Normal: any licking of the areas, swelling, discharge, odor, inability to urinate

Perineum – *Examine the area under the tail area*

Normal: clean and dry, no swelling
Not Normal: swelling, discharge, odor, scooting, licking

Tail – *Examine the pet's tail*

Normal: able to hold tail upright, wag tail
Not Normal: inability to move tail, growths, swelling, pain, crooked tail, open wounds

SENIOR PETS

Our pets are loyal for many years. With improved veterinary care, our pets are living longer lives. As they age, age-related conditions arise which may include:

- arthritis
- kidney/liver/and urinary disease
- weakness
- senility
- diabetes
- heart disease
- cancer
- vision and hearing loss

SIGNS OF AGING

Signs that may be observed in our senior pets include:

- signs of pain when getting up from resting
- difficulty going up and down steps
- increase in the times they need to go out to urinate/defecate
- soiling in the house when they did not before
- confusion
- sleeping more
- exaggerated reactions to sounds
- bumping into objects
- not hearing being called or sensing danger outside
- an increase in anxiety
- a decrease in the ability to keep themselves clean
- repetitive activity
- wandering
- an increase in the chance of skin growths and other cancers
- loss of appetite

TIPS FOR AGING PETS

What to do for our senior pets:

- watch their physical activity
- keep as active as they are able without overdoing it
- medicate if in pain/discomfort
- consider their dietary needs as they age
- observe their eating habits
- visit the veterinarian at least twice a year
- treat conditions that develop as soon as possible
- consider routine blood work to identify disorders early
- senior-proof your home—watch for furniture that may cause harm if bumped into, close off stairs, use ramps, make food and water bowls accessible
- be aware of vision or hearing loss
- monitor the pet's dental health
- protect the senior pets from temperature changes
- use soft blankets for comfort
- use rugs and carpeted areas for ease of walking and rising as needed
- cherish every moment—time goes very fast when we love our pets

DOG AGES

GENERAL AGES OF PETS COMPARED TO HUMAN YEARS ARE:

DOG	HUMAN
6–12 months	10–15 years
12–18 months	15–20 years
18–24 months	20–24 years
4 years	32 years
6 years	40 years
8 years	48 years
10–12 years	56–64 years
13–14 years	68–72 years
15–20 years	76–96 years

DOGS SIZES:

Small dogs age more slowly than large-breed dogs

Small-sized dogs: 0–20 pounds

Medium-sized dogs: 21–50 pounds

Large-sized dogs: 5–90 pounds

Very large-sized dogs: over 90 pounds

THE END

This may be the end of this book, but it is really never the end. There is always more to learn and share.

www.ingramcontent.com/pod-product-compliance
Lightning Source LLC
Chambersburg PA
CBHW050858240426
43673CB00009B/280